Answers to DIFFICULT BIBLE TEXTS

by
Joe Crews

Roseville CA

Printed in the USA
All Rights Reserved

Published by Amazing Facts, Inc.
P.O. Box 1058
Roseville CA 95678
800-538-7275

Cover Design by Haley Trimmer
Text Design by Greg Solie • AltamontGraphics.com

ISBN 978-1-58019-008-4

TABLE OF CONTENTS

INDEX

Genesis 9:3

"Every moving thing that liveth shall be meat for you; even as the green herb have I given you all things."

Before the Flood, God gave no permission for man to eat the flesh of animals. The original diet laid down in Genesis 1:29 and 3:18 consisted of nuts, fruits, grains, and vegetables. This order of things prevailed until after the Flood. Then, because vegetation had been destroyed by the Flood, God allowed the use of flesh food for the first time. It was for this purpose that the clean animals had been taken into the ark by sevens and the unclean by twos (Genesis 7:1, 2).

Even though Genesis 9:3 seems to be an unrestricted permit to eat any kind of animal, please note that it was not without limits. God said, "Even as the green herb have I given you all things." In the same way that God had given vegetation, so now He gave flesh. But all vegetation was not good to eat. There were weeds and poisonous plants that could not be eaten. In the same way, God proceeded soon afterward (Leviticus ch. 11) to show that certain animals were not good for food and should definitely not be eaten.

It is also interesting to note that this instruction was given to Noah immediately after leaving the ark. Since it takes two (both male and female) to propagate a species and only two of each unclean animal were saved in the ark, it is certain that God did not give license to eat the unclean animals. If He had, the unclean species would have been exterminated, and none would exist today.

Genesis 35:18

"And it came to pass, as her soul was in departing, (for she died) that she called his name Benoni: but his father called him Benjamin."

Since it is not possible for souls to exist outside of bodies, how do we explain this apparent contradiction? The word "soul" is translated from the Hebrew word "nephesh" which has been translated 118 times in the Old Testament as "life." The same word is used in Genesis 1:30 in reference to animals. It is never used in one single instance to denote an immortal or undying part of man.

Exodus 4:21

"And the Lord said unto Moses, When thou goest to return into Egypt, see that thou do all those wonders before Pharaoh, which I have put in thine hand: but I will harden his heart, that he shall not let the people go."

It is a fascinating fact that the Hebrew word "chazaq" is translated as "hardened" in almost every account of God's dealing with Pharaoh. But when Pharaoh "hardened" his own heart, the Hebrew word "kabed" is used. Why this difference?

Actually the word "chazaq" has a literal meaning of "strengthen, courage." For example, we read in 1 Samuel 30:6 that "David encouraged himself in the Lord," but the word translated "encouraged" is "chazaq"—the same word which is translated as "hardened" in this passage. "Chazaq" is also translated as "encouraged" in the following verses: Deuteronomy 1:38; 2 Samuel 11:25; 2 Chronicles 35:2; Psalm 64:5; Isaiah 41:7; Deuteronomy 3:28; Judges 20:22; 2 Chronicles 31:4.

When we take the true meaning of the word, we find that God actually encouraged Pharaoh's heart to let Israel go. But when Pharaoh hardened his own heart, the Bible uses a different word—"kabed"—which means "to make heavy, harden" (Exodus 8:15).

But why did the "encouragement" of the Lord have the effect of hardening Pharaoh's heart? We might just as well ask why the same encouraging, inspiring ministry of Jesus could produce a loving John and a traitorous Judas. One was softened, and the other was hardened. The same sun that softens the wax will harden the clay. Every man is exposed in some degree to the grace of Christ (John 1:9). The Lord is spoken of as a sun (Psalm 84:11) who lightens every man. Some reject the light and grow hard (Zechariah 7:12). Some accept and are softened. The end result depends on the response of each individual.

Exodus 16:29

"See, for that the LORD hath given you the sabbath, therefore he giveth you on the sixth day the bread of two days; abide ye every man in his place, let no man go out of his place on the seventh day."

Many overlook the fact that this command applied only to gathering manna. "Let no man go out of his place on the seventh day" must be linked with God's words in verse 25: "Today is a sabbath unto the LORD: today ye shall not find it in the field." When some did go out to gather on the seventh day, God met them with a rebuke for breaking His law (verses 27, 28).

This text does not forbid all travel on the Sabbath, as some seek to establish. Bible examples demonstrate that proper travel was considered lawful on the day (2 Kings 4:23). Even Christ traveled to church on the Sabbath without breaking it (Luke 4:16).

Exodus 20:4

"Thou shalt not make unto thee any graven image, or any likeness of anything that is in heaven above, or that is in the earth beneath, or that is in the water under the earth."

After the first commandment designates the true God, the second teaches how He is to be worshiped. This commandment specifically forbids the veneration of objects representing God. "Thou shalt not bow down thyself to them, nor serve them" (Exodus 20:5). Please take note that it is the veneration or worship of the graven form which constitutes sin.

This text does not forbid religious illustration, photography, or the fine arts. God Himself gave command for carved angels in the most holy place (Exodus 25:18), embroidered angels in the tabernacle hangings (1 Kings 6:29) and cast bronze oxen in the courtyard (1 Kings 7:25).

The Lord also instructed Moses to fashion a brazen serpent in the wilderness (Numbers 21:8, 9). There was nothing wrong with it as an illustrative device pointing the people to faith in their healing God. Yet the same bronze serpent was ordered destroyed when it became an object of worship and veneration by the backslidden nation (2 Kings 18:4). This proves that a carved form is not sin in itself. It only becomes evil when used as an object of adoration.

Exodus 34:28

"And he was there with the Lord forty days and forty nights; he did neither eat bread, nor drink water. And he wrote upon the tables the words of the covenant, the ten commandments."

The grammatical structure of this verse makes it seem that Moses might have written the Ten Commandments on the second set of stone tablets. "And he was there with the Lord … and he wrote upon the tables." The important thing to note here is that the second "he" does not refer to Moses, but to the Lord. In verse 1, God said plainly to Moses, "Hew thee two tables of stone *like unto the first*: and I will write upon these tables the words that were in the first tables, which thou brakest."

In Deuteronomy 10:2-4, the record is even more specific. The Lord said, "I will write on the tables the words that were in the first tables … And he wrote on the tables, according to the first writing, the ten commandments."

Moses did not do any writing on tables of stone. He wrote the ordinances and ceremonial law in a book, but that was entirely different from the moral law in the stone tablets.

Even though the Ten Commandment law is called a "covenant," it was not the old covenant which vanished away at the death of Jesus. (For further explanation of the Ten Commandments as a covenant, see my comments on Deuteronomy 4:13 and Hebrews 8:7, 8.)

Leviticus 3:17

"It shall be a perpetual statute for your generations throughout all your dwellings, that ye eat neither fat nor blood."

On the basis of this text, some have taken a position against blood transfusions. But the position is entirely untenable in the light of these considerations:

1. The prohibition applied only to animal blood and fowls (Leviticus 7:25-27). It does not apply to humans because we don't eat humans.

2. God gave proper instruction for slaughtering an animal or fowl so as not to eat any blood (Leviticus 17:13, 14).

3. God's prohibition against eating blood also applies to Christians (Acts 15:20).

4. That which is eaten goes through the digestion into the stomach (Matthew 15:17). Blood transfusions go directly to the veins and thence to the cells.

5. If we love our neighbor as ourselves, can we watch him die for lack of life-giving blood (Matthew 22:39)?

6. Jesus came to save men's lives (Luke 9:56); why shouldn't we?

7. Since the life is in the blood (Deuteronomy 12:23), Christ condoned the giving of blood to save a life (John 15:13).

Numbers 15:32, 35

"And while the children of Israel were in the wilderness, they found a man that gathered sticks upon the sabbath day. ... And the LORD said unto Moses, The man shall be surely put to death: all the congregation shall stone him with stones without the camp."

Some have made a big point that Sabbathbreakers were stoned to death in the Old Testament, therefore the Sabbath must not be in force today since stoning is not in force. But take note that not only Sabbathbreakers were stoned to death, but adulterers as well (Leviticus 20:10). Those also who broke the second commandment were put to death (Leviticus 24:16). Surely no one feels that adultery and blasphemy are any less wrong today just because God prescribed death for such sins in the Old Testament.

The fact is that under the theocracy of Israel, God ruled the people directly. He commanded punishment immediately for certain flagrant acts of disobedience. Today the same sins are equally abhorrent to God, but punishment is delayed until the day of judgment.

Deuteronomy 4:13

"And he declared unto you his covenant, which he commanded you to perform, even ten commandments; and he wrote them upon two tables of stone."

The dispensationalist doctrine makes the Ten Commandment law the old covenant that was abolished. Even though the Ten Commandments were indeed a commanded covenant, they did not constitute the old covenant which vanished away (Hebrews 8:13). Here are the reasons:

1. The old covenant was faulty, had poor promises, and vanished away (Hebrews 8:7, 8, 13). None of those points apply to the perfect law of God (Psalm 19:7).

2. The old covenant was made "concerning all these words" of the written law (Exodus 24:7, 8). It was not the law itself.

3. Referring to the Ten Commandments, God said to Moses, "… for after the tenor of these words I have made a covenant with thee and with Israel" (Exodus 34:27, 28). It was not the law itself but over the keeping of the law—"the tenor of the words"—that the old covenant was made.

4. Moses referred to the golden calf as "your sin, the calf which ye had made…" (Deuteronomy 9:21). (Please note: The calf was not the sin, but the sin took place concerning the calf.) In the same way, the old covenant was not the law, but it was concerning the law. Thus it is called the covenant.

5. Romans 9:4 proves that the old and new covenants were different from the law itself: "Who are Israelites; to whom pertaineth the adoption,

and the glory, and the covenants, and the giving of the law…" Here the law is mentioned, as well as the covenants (plural). This would include both old and new covenants, plus the "giving of the law," which is the Ten Commandment law.

6. To prove positively that the law is not the old covenant, let's try to make the words interchangeable in Romans 3:31: "Do we then make void the (old covenant) law through faith? God forbid: yea, we establish the (old covenant) law." Clearly the old covenant and the law are not the same.

Deuteronomy 5:2, 3

"The LORD our God made a covenant with us in Horeb. The LORD made not this covenant with our fathers, but with us, even us, who are all of us here alive this day."

Since the basis of this covenant was the Ten Commandments, as revealed in verses 6-21, some people contend that the decalogue was never applied to anyone before the law was written at Sinai. But such a conclusion is not valid on the basis of the words of Moses to the people of Israel. He was not telling them that there had been no previous agreement about obeying the law. There had been covenants with individuals who indeed had been their forefathers, but only on a *personal* basis.

At Sinai, for the very first time, God entered into a covenant relationship with *an entire nation*. And it was that specific covenant which had never existed before. Moses could truthfully say that "this covenant" was not made "with our fathers," but only with those leaders who accepted God's offer at Horeb—those who were still alive at that very time.

Deuteronomy 5:3, 4

"The LORD made not this covenant with our fathers, but with us, even us, who are all of us here alive this day. The LORD talked with you face to face in the mount out of the midst of the fire."

Some conclude from this text that the Ten Commandments were not known before the written law at Mount Sinai. However, the evidence is all to the contrary. Cain knew it was a sin to murder. Joseph called adultery a sin, and God said, "Abraham obeyed my voice, and kept my charge, my commandments, my statutes and my laws" (Genesis 26:5).

In these verses, Moses is impressing upon them the solemn fact of God's visit with them on Sinai, and the covenant law He delivered to them. Moses said, "The LORD talked with you face to face"—something He had not done with their fathers. The fathers were dead; they had not seen the mountain smoke; they had not heard the majestic voice of God speak the law. "The LORD made not this covenant with our fathers, but with us, even us, who are all of us here alive this day."

This does not mean that their fathers had not been acquainted with the provisions of the covenant. They simply had not had the covenant terms spelled out in written form before them. Many years later, Jeremiah reminded the leaders of Israel about the law covenant at Sinai. He reminded them that God said this is the covenant "Which I commanded your fathers in the day that I brought them forth out of the land of Egypt, … saying, Obey my voice, … That I may perform the oath which I have sworn unto your fathers, to give them a land flowing with milk and honey …" (Jeremiah 11:4, 5). So obviously their fathers had received the promise in the everlasting covenant, but not face to face, as at Sinai.

Proof positive that the covenant had been made known to the fathers of those who left Egypt is found in 1 Chronicles 16:15-17: "Be ye mindful always of his covenant … Even of the covenant which he made with Abraham, and of his oath unto Isaac; And hath confirmed the same to Jacob for a law, and to Israel for an everlasting covenant." Please notice that the covenant had been revealed to Abraham, Isaac, and Jacob "for a law" long before it was written on stone at Sinai.

In Deuteronomy 29, the covenant is repeated again with the reminder that it had been sworn to Abraham, Isaac, and Jacob. Then follow these words: "Neither with you only do I make this covenant and this oath; But with him that standeth here with us this day before the LORD our God, and also with him that is not here with us this day" (verses 14, 15).

Deuteronomy 5:14, 15

"*But the seventh day is the sabbath of the LORD thy God: in it thou shalt not do any work, thou, nor thy son, nor thy daughter, nor thy manservant, nor thy maidservant, nor thine ox, nor thine ass, nor any of thy cattle, nor thy stranger that is within thy gates; that thy manservant and thy maidservant may rest as well as thou. And remember that thou wast a servant in the land of Egypt, and that the LORD thy God brought thee out thence through a mighty hand and by a stretched out arm: therefore the LORD thy God commanded thee to keep the sabbath day.*"

Some people draw from this text that God gave the Sabbath as a memorial of the exodus from Egypt. But the Genesis story of the making of the Sabbath (Genesis 2:1-3) and the wording of the fourth commandment by God Himself (Exodus 20:11) reveals the Sabbath as a memorial of creation.

The key to understanding these two verses rests in the word "servant." God said, "Remember that thou wast a servant in the land of Egypt." And in the sentence before this one, He reminded them "that thy manservant and thy maidservant may rest as well as thou." In other words, their experience in Egypt as servants would remind them to deal justly with their servants by giving them Sabbath rest.

In a similar vein, God had commanded, "And if a stranger sojourn with thee in your land, ye shall not vex him … for ye were strangers in the land of Egypt …" (Leviticus 19:33, 34).

It was not unusual for God to hark back to the Egyptian deliverance as an incentive to obey other commandments. In Deuteronomy 24:17, 18, God said, "Thou shalt not pervert the judgment of the stranger, nor of the fatherless; nor take a widow's raiment to pledge … thou wast a bondman in Egypt and the LORD thy God redeemed thee thence: therefore I command thee to do this thing."

Neither the command to be just nor the command to keep the Sabbath was given to memorialize the exodus, but God told them that His goodness in bringing them out of captivity constituted a strong *additional* reason for their dealing kindly with their servants on the Sabbath and treating justly the strangers and widows.

In the same vein, God spoke to them in Leviticus 11:45: "For I am the Lord that bringeth you up out of the land of Egypt, ... ye shall therefore be holy ..." Surely no one would insist that holiness did not exist before the exodus, or that it would be ever afterwards limited only to the Jews, to memorialize their deliverance.

Deuteronomy 14:21

"Ye shall not eat of any thing that dieth of itself: thou shalt give it unto the stranger that is in thy gates, that he may eat it; or thou mayest sell it unto an alien: for thou art an holy people unto the Lord thy God. Thou shalt not seethe a kid in his mother's milk."

God's people were not to touch any clean beast which died of itself, or to eat its flesh, else they would be "unclean" until sundown (Leviticus 11:39, 40). These laws did not apply to the non-Jews, so the dead animals could be sold to them with no ceremonial uncleanness involved. Even the Jews were considered clean again after sunset.

Deuteronomy 14:26

"And thou shalt bestow that money for whatsoever thy soul lusteth after, for oxen, or for sheep, or for wine, or for strong drink, or for whatsoever thy soul desireth: and thou shalt eat there before the Lord thy God, and thou shalt rejoice, thou, and thine household."

The context of this verse is needed to clarify the thought of the writer. It is apparent from verse 22 that he is talking about the use of the second tithe: "Thou shalt truly tithe all the increase." The first tithe had already been specifically allotted to the Levites (Numbers 18:21, 24). Some of this second tithe was to be given to the strangers, the orphans and the widows (Deuteronomy 14:29; 26:12-15).

In verse 23, God told the Israelites to journey to the place He would designate and present the tithe to Him there—no doubt, at the tabernacle. In verses 24 and 25, they were permitted to change the corn, cattle, etc., into the equivalent cash if the way was too long to travel with produce and herds.

In verse 26, God gave instruction for the money to be turned back into an offering for Him after reaching the holy place. But instead of prescribing the exact offering, He told them they could present whatever they desired. Some have been confused by God's listing strong drink among the other offerings that they were permitted. But please notice that this wine was not to be drunk—it was to be poured out as an offering before the Lord. God described the act in Numbers 28:7: "In the holy place shalt thou cause the strong wine to be poured unto the LORD for a drink offering."

Take note that all the items suggested by God for the money to be invested in were offerings for Him. Some have stumbled over the wording, "whatsoever thy soul lusteth after" and "whatsoever thy soul desireth." Remember that God is talking to His faithful people who are tithing. He assumes that they are not going to desire evil things as an offering to Him. The Psalmist said, "Delight thyself also in the LORD; and he shall give thee the desires of thine heart" (Psalm 37:4). For God's people, those desires would be their own choice of acceptable offerings and gifts to present to their Lord.

Deuteronomy 23:18

"Thou shalt not bring the hire of a whore, or the price of a dog, into the house of the LORD thy God for any vow: for even both these are abomination unto the LORD thy God."

The term "dog" is used in the Hebrew idiom for a male prostitute. It refers back to the "sodomite" of verse 17. It is the male equivalent of the female whore or harlot. In Eastern countries, the dog has ever been a half-wild, mangy, disagreeable animal which symbolizes uncleanness. The "hire" or "price" gained from such illicit practice was not to be dedicated to God's work.

The New Testament also uses the term in the same sense as representing the outcasts and sinners. Revelation 22:15 speaks of those outside the New Jerusalem as "dogs, and sorcerers, and whoremongers," etc. Paul admonishes the Philippians to "Beware of dogs, beware of evil workers ..." (Philippians 3:2).

1 Samuel 28:14

"And he said unto her, What form is he of? And she said, An old man cometh up; and he is covered with a mantle. And Saul perceived that it was Samuel, and he stooped with his face to the ground, and bowed himself"

This spiritual séance has been cited as evidence for life after death. But here are points to the contrary:

1.   Wizards had been sentenced to death or banned from the land (1 Samuel 28:3; Leviticus 20:27).
2.   God had departed from Saul and would not communicate with him (1 Samuel 28:15).
3.   Samuel was supposedly "brought up." Other expressions used in this passage include: "ascending out of the earth," "cometh up," and "bring ... up" (verses 13-15). Is this where the righteous dead are—down in the earth? Not according to those who believe in the immortal soul.
4.   Samuel is described as an old man covered with a mantle. Is this the way immortal souls appear? And where did the soul get the body? They're supposed to be disembodied. Was there a resurrection? Did God obey the beck and call of the witch and raise up Samuel? If not, can Satan raise the dead?
5.   The apparition of Samuel told Saul, "... tomorrow shalt thou and thy sons be with me ..." (1 Samuel 28:19). Saul committed suicide on the battlefield the next day. Where did Samuel dwell, if the wicked Saul was to go to the same place?

6. The Bible never says that Saul saw Samuel. He received his information secondhand from the witch, and only concluded it was Samuel from her description. The truth is that the devil deceived the dissolute old woman, and she deceived Saul. It was nothing more than a devil-generated séance.

7. The enormity of Saul's sin is revealed in these words: "So Saul died for his transgression … and also for asking counsel of one that had a familiar spirit, to enquire of it; And enquired not of the Lord: therefore he slew him …" (1 Chronicles 10:13, 14).

2 Samuel 7:15, 16

"But my mercy shall not depart away from him, as I took it from Saul, whom I put away before thee. And thine house and thy kingdom shall be established for ever before thee: thy throne shall be established for ever."

The British Israel theory advocates use these verses to support their contention that God made an unconditional promise to David that his throne, his house, and his kingdom would never fail, regardless of their faithfulness or unfaithfulness. The theory is unsound and false in the light of these texts, which declare the promise to be conditional:

1. 1 Kings 9:4-7: "If thou wilt walk before me … in uprightness … and wilt keep my statutes and my judgments: Then I will establish the throne of thy kingdom upon Israel for ever, as I promised to David…. But if ye shall at all turn from following me, … Then will I cut off Israel … and this house, … will I cast out."

2. 1 Kings 2:4: "… If thy children … walk before me in truth… there shall not fail thee … a man on the throne of Israel."

3. I Kings 6:12: "… if thou wilt walk in my statutes then will I perform my word with thee, which I spake unto David thy father."

4. 1 Chronicles 28:7: "Moreover I will establish his kingdom for ever, if he be constant to do my commandments and my judgments."
5. 2 Chronicles 7:17, 18: "… if thou wilt walk before me, as David thy father walked, … Then will I stablish the throne …."
6. Psalm 132:11, 12: "The LORD hath sworn in truth unto David; he will not turn from it; Of the fruit of thy body will I set upon thy throne. If thy children will keep my covenant … their children shall also sit upon thy throne for evermore."

The theory is further proven unsound by these undeniable facts:

1. The word "forever" does not always mean "without end." (See my comments on Revelation 14:10, 11.)
2. The fleshly Israel was completely disqualified because of their disobedience (Romans 4:13; 9:7, 8; 11:20).
3. Christ's spiritual rule fulfilled the promise concerning David's throne (Acts 2:29, 30; Isaiah 9:6, 7).
4. The kingdom was taken from the nation of Israel (Matthew 21:43) and given to another nation (1 Peter 2:9, 10).
5. Israel's house was left desolate (Matthew 23:38).
6. All who are Christ's may now claim the promises of God's spiritual Israel (Galatians 3:29; Romans 11:17).

1 Kings 17:21, 22

"And he stretched himself upon the child three times, and cried unto the LORD, and said, O LORD my God, I pray thee, let this child's soul come into him again. And the LORD heard the voice of Elijah; and the soul of the child came into him again, and he revived."

Since it is not possible for souls to exist outside of bodies, how do we explain this apparent contradiction? The word "soul" is translated from the Hebrew word "nephesh" which has been translated 118 times in the Old Testament as "life." The same word is used in Genesis 1:30 in reference to animals. It is never used in one single instance to denote an immortal or undying part of man.

Every conflict is harmonized if the more proper word "life" is used in reference to the child, instead of "soul." His life slipped away, or left the body. Then the life returned to the boy when the prophet prayed.

Don't overlook the fact that the lifeless body was called "him" as well as the restored boy. This proves that the "person" did not depart to be with the Lord. The whole person was represented by the body, whether dead or alive.

Nehemiah 9:14

"And madest known unto them thy holy sabbath, and commandedst them precepts, statutes, and laws, by the hand of Moses thy servant."

Does this text imply that the Sabbath was not in existence before it was revealed at Mount Sinai? Definitely not! It had only been forgotten, and needed to be made known to those who no longer knew it.

Compare Ezekiel 20:5 and the meaning becomes crystal clear. God said, "In the day when I chose Israel … and made myself known unto them in the land of Egypt …" This certainly doesn't mean that God did not exist before. They had forgotten His existence, just as they had forgotten the Sabbath, and both had to be made known to them in Egypt and at Sinai.

Job 14:21, 22

"His sons come to honor, and he knoweth it not; and they are brought low, but he perceiveth it not of them. But his flesh upon him shall have pain, and his soul within him shall mourn."

Verse 22 appears to be saying that a dead man's fleshly body can continue to give him pain and that his soul can be grieved. Although it is obvious to all that the bodily sensations cease at death, a closer look at these poetic words reveal their true meaning. It must be remembered that in Hebrew poetry, intelligence, personality and feelings are often ascribed to objects or concepts that do not normally have these attributes (Judges 9:8-15). Job is actually describing, in a very graphic way, the ravages that take place at death. As a body decays, its horrible state of decomposition contorts all the physical features into the expression of grimacing pain.

The New English Bible transposes verses 21 and 22 and correctly translates the passage this way: "His flesh upon him becomes black, and his life-blood dries up within him. His sons rise to honor, and he sees nothing of it; they sink into obscurity, and he knows it not."

In verse 12, the state of man in death is fully clarified: "So man lieth down, and riseth not: till the heavens be no more, they shall not awake, nor be raised out of their sleep." Thus the writer of Job agrees perfectly with the words of Christ, who later described death as an unconscious sleep (John 11:11).

Job 34:14, 15

"If he set his heart upon man, if he gather unto himself his spirit and his breath; All flesh shall perish together, and man shall turn again unto dust."

This text points back to Creation, when God "breathed into his (man's) nostrils the breath of life; and man became a living soul" (Genesis 2:7). In many other texts of Scripture, the breath which entered man's nostrils is identified as the "spirit." In Job 27:3 we read, "All the while my breath is in me, and the spirit of God is in my nostrils." Genesis, of course, describes breath going into the nostrils at the time of creation, not the spirit; but the Hebrew parallelism of Job 27:3 repeats the same thought in a secondary phrase, calling the breath in the nostrils the "spirit of God in my nostrils."

The Psalmist, on the other hand, describes the same process in these words: "Thou sendest forth thy spirit, they are created." "Thou takest away their breath, they die, and return to their dust" (Psalm 104:30, 29). These texts show how the words "breath" and "spirit" are used interchangeably in the Bible. Sometimes it says that God created by putting His breath into the body, but again it will say He created by putting the spirit into the body. Incidentally, death is described not only as "breath" returning to God (Psalm 104:29), but also as the "spirit" returning to God (Ecclesiastes 12:7).

Our text in Job 34:14, 15 now begins to come into focus, as it describes the process by which man dies and "shall turn again unto dust." In this case, since the reference is not to an individual dying, but rather to the death of "all flesh," the Psalmist employs a parallel use of both words, "breath" and "spirit," to describe the removal of the life principle.

Proverbs 31:6

"Give strong drink unto him that is ready to perish, and wine unto those that be of heavy hearts."

This text and its preceding verses plainly reveal that no intelligent individual with a good mind will use intoxicating beverages. With no drugs to deaden the pain of a fatal illness, the ancients used strong drink as a pain-killing agent along with certain narcotic herbs (Matthew 27:34). The Amplified Old Testament reads, "Give strong drink (as medicine) to him."

In the same sense, wine was allowed for the manic depressive, just as tranquilizing agents are used today. The Amplified Bible reads, "… wine to those in bitter distress of heart …" —a clear description of severe emotional sickness. But the same writer strongly urges that responsible people not be given any wine (verses 4, 5).

Isaiah 35:9

"No lion shall be there, nor any ravenous beast shall go up thereon, it shall not be found there, but the redeemed shall walk there."

The thought of this text is that "no ravenous beast" will be in the new earth to hurt or destroy (Isaiah 65:25). The lions will be as gentle as lambs (Isaiah 11:6-9). The prophet Ezekiel clarifies the picture with these words: "The LORD will cause the evil beasts to cease out of the land" (Ezekiel 34:24, 25). Lions there will be tame enough for a child to lead (Isaiah 11:6).

Isaiah 65:20

"There shall be no more thence an infant of days, nor an old man that hath not filled his days. for the child shall die an hundred years old; but the sinner being an hundred years old shall be accursed."

This text has perplexed Bible students for generations. The awkward wording seems to imply that even death might still plague the saints in God's new world of tomorrow. Some have taken the context to indicate a subjunctive form of speech in the translation. This would indicate that the prophet was using a human terminology to describe heavenly conditions. In other words, Isaiah was saying, "Should (or if) certain conditions prevail, then such and such would result." This translation seems to give the closest to the original meaning if the subjunctive sense is accepted:

"There shall be no child to arise or come into being who shall live only a certain number of days. If it were possible that there be still sinners in Jerusalem (there won't be) and if one of them should be punished with death when 100 years old, he would be regarded as cursed by God and forever cut off from mercy. And if one should die a natural death at 100 (which he won't) he would still be a boy."

Isaiah was seeking to illustrate the facts of eternal life in heaven by earthly comparisons. Therefore he had to call on his readers to imagine certain mortal conditions as being in the new earth, so that they could grasp the truths of immortality.

Isaiah 66:24

"And they shall go forth, and look upon the carcases of the men that have transgressed against me: for their worm shall not die, neither shall their fire be quenched; and they shall be an abhorring unto all flesh."

This description of the final destruction of the wicked assures us that they finally are lifeless "carcases" (dead bodies). Their bodies burn in the lake of fire. (See my comments on Mark 9:43, 44 for an explanation of the undying worm and unquenchable fire.)

Since the walls of the holy city will be "clear as crystal" (Revelation 21:11, 18), the redeemed might easily go forth from their heavenly homes, look through the crystal-clear walls, and "see the reward of the wicked" (Psalm 91:8). This certainly will not be a very pleasant spectacle. Zechariah 14:12 says: "Their flesh shall consume away …" But the wicked soon are burned up (Malachi 4:1, 3) and shall be as though they had not been (Obadiah 16). Then the earth is recreated as the eternal home of the righteous, all tears are wiped away, and there shall be no more pain (Revelation 21:1, 4).

Jeremiah 10:1-6

"Hear ye the word which the Lord speaketh unto you, O house of Israel: Thus saith the Lord, Learn not the way of the heathen, and be not dismayed at the signs of heaven; for the heathen are dismayed at them. For the customs of the people are vain: for one cutteth a tree out of the forest, the work of the hands of the workman, with the axe. They deck it with silver and with gold; they fasten it with nails and with hammers, that it move not. They are upright as the palm tree, but speak not: they must needs be borne, because they cannot go. Be not afraid of them; for they cannot do evil, neither also is it in them to do good. Forasmuch as there is none like unto thee, O Lord; thou art great, and thy name is great in might."

This text has been used as condemnation of Christmas trees, and a casual reading sounds as though the writer had the modem Christmas decorations in mind. But the context of the chapter places a different meaning upon the words.

Jeremiah is describing the ways of the heathen in cutting a tree from the forest and carving an idol which is worshiped as a god. In verse 14, he speaks of the "graven image" as a false god: "there is no breath in them." In verses 10-12, "The gods that have not made the heavens and the earth" are contrasted with the creative power of the true God.

After the tree is cut and shaped with the axe, Jeremiah says that it is decorated and fastened with nails (verses 3,4). There it remains, dumb and unheeding. It cannot speak or walk (verse 5). To worship the "stock" of a tree is "brutish and foolish" (verse 8). Even though it is covered with silver plate and delicate clothing, it remains a "doctrine of vanities" (verses 8, 9).

Jeremiah 17:27

"But if ye will not hearken unto me to hallow the sabbath day, and not to bear a burden, even entering in at the gates of Jerusalem on the sabbath day; then will I kindle a fire in the gates thereof and it shall devour the palaces of Jerusalem, and it shall not be quenched."

The fire which "devoured the palaces of Jerusalem" is spoken of in this text as fire which "shall not be quenched." This does not mean that the fire could never go out, but that it could never be "quenched" or "put out" before it had accomplished its purpose. It was a strange fire which God kindled and man could not control or extinguish. The same fire is described in 2 Chronicles 36:19 and the results recorded: "And they burnt the house of God, and brake down the wall of Jerusalem, and burnt all the palaces thereof with fire, and destroyed all the goodly vessels thereof."

That fire is not still burning. It burned itself out, even though it could not be quenched by man. The same kind of fire will destroy the wicked in the lake of fire and brimstone, according to Mark 9:44, 45. If the wicked could quench the fire, they could escape from it. But Isaiah wrote, "They shall not deliver themselves from the power of the flame: there shall not be a coal to warm at, nor fire to sit before it" (Isaiah 47:14). Notice that the last part of this verse provides further evidence that it will go out completely after consuming the bodies of the wicked.

Jeremiah 31:15-17

"Thus saith the LORD, A voice was heard in Ramah, lamentation, and bitter weeping; Rachel weeping for her children refused to be comforted for her children, because they were not. Thus saith the LORD; Refrain thy voice from weeping, and thine eyes from tears; for thy work shall be rewarded, saith the LORD; and they shall come again from the land of the enemy. And there is hope in thine end, saith the LORD, that thy children shall come again to their own border."

Matthew applies this prophecy to the slaying of the children by Herod in his attempt to destroy Jesus (Matthew 2:17, 18). This is one of the verses of the Bible which gives assurance that babes will be saved in God's kingdom. "They shall come again from the land of the enemy." Those children slain by Herod were two years of age or under, and not yet accountable for sin.

Sometimes a mistaken application is made of Obadiah 16 to infants and children—that they will be as though they had not been. There is no such meaning in the context. It has reference to the nations of the wicked who will be eternally destroyed, and possibly to certain groups of unlearned heathen who will not be punished for their state of sinful ignorance. Children are definitely not specified in that text.

Deuteronomy 1:39 indicates that God accepts the children who are not old enough to understand about sin. "Moreover your little ones, which ye said should be a prey, and your children, which in that day had no knowledge between good and evil, they shall go in thither, and unto them will I give it, and they shall possess it." The children were allowed to go into the promised land with faithful Caleb and Joshua. This is a type of entrance into the heavenly Canaan. Jesus used little children as an example of the experience all must attain in order to enter the kingdom of heaven (Matthew 18:3).

Ezekiel 16:11-13

"I decked thee also with ornaments, and I put bracelets upon thy hands, and a chain on thy neck. And I put a jewel on thy forehead, and earrings in thine ears, and a beautiful crown upon thine head. Thus wast thou decked with gold and silver; and thy raiment was of fine linen, and silk, and embroidered work; thou didst eat fine flour, and honey, and oil: and thou wast exceeding beautiful, and thou didst prosper into a kingdom."

This text seems to conflict with scores of other verses which condemn the use of colorful cosmetics and jewelry. Yet there is no real conflict if the context is considered. This is not a literal experience, but a symbolism. In verse 3, God begins the recital of a moving allegory concerning His people Israel. He depicts Israel being born illegitimately and cast into a field to die. No one washed the baby or cared for it. Then God passed by and loved the baby. He covered its nakedness and washed away its filth. He bestowed upon it love and every possible blessing.

In allegorizing the material and spiritual blessings that He bestowed on Israel, God used a number of symbols which are clearly interpreted by other Bible writers. The "fine linen" of verse 10 is defined in Revelation 19:8: "The fine linen is the righteousness of saints." The ornaments and chain of verse 11 are interpreted in Proverbs 1:9 as the "ornament of grace." The jewel and crown of verse 12 are symbolic of "lips of knowledge" (Proverbs 20:15), and a "crown of rejoicing" (I Thessalonians 2:19), respectively. All the representations of highest honor, recognition, wealth, and beauty were incorporated in the allegory to show the unparalleled blessings which Israel had received as a nation.

The symbolic ornaments of this allegory in no way mitigate the force of those texts forbidding the actual display of such vanity on the physical body.

Ezekiel 36:25, 26

"Then will I sprinkle clean water upon you, and ye shall be clean: from all your filthiness, and from all your idols, will I cleanse you. A new heart also will I give you, and a new spirit will I put within you: and I will take away the stony heart out of your flesh, and I will give you an heart of flesh."

There is a popular contention that these verses prefigure the introduction of sprinkling for baptism. A few facts reveal that it had no connection with the later Christian ordinance:

1. Moses was instructed to set the Levites apart for the priesthood. God said, "Sprinkle water of purifying upon them" (Numbers 8:7).

2. Certain unclean people—such as those who touched a dead body (Numbers 19:16-18), or a menstruating woman (Leviticus 15:19)—were isolated until they had been sprinkled with water of purification (Numbers 19:13). Ashes of a heifer were also used in connection with the sprinkled water (Numbers 19:17-19).

3. In Ezekiel 36:25, 26, God does the sprinkling, and not man to another man. He compares His people to the defiled or unclean of Israel and uses a term of cleansing they could understand.

4. Sprinkling was done away with under the new covenant along with ashes of a heifer, etc. "Neither by the blood of goats and calves, but by his own blood he ... obtained eternal redemption for us. For if the blood of bulls and of goats, and the ashes of an heifer sprinkling the unclean, sanctifieth to the purifying of the flesh: How much more shall the blood of Christ ... purge your conscience ..." (Hebrews 9:12-14).

5. There is no scriptural connection whatsoever between the ceremonial sprinkling of the Old Testament and the New Testament ordinance of baptism, an act of complete immersion (Romans 6:4-6).

Amos 5:23

"Take thou away from me the noise of thy songs; for I will not hear the melody of thy viols."

Those who believe it wrong to use musical instruments in worship base some of their doctrine on this text. Yet the same condemnation is made of "solemn assemblies" in verse 21. Would they ban the "solemn assemblies" as they do the "melody of thy viols"?

God is here showing His disgust for the hypocritical practice of religious forms while dividing their service with heathen gods (verse 26).

Several texts of the Bible indicate that musical instruments may be a glory to God, on earth as well as in heaven. "As well the singers as the players on instruments shall be there ..." (Psalm 87:7). This refers to Zion, the church—the place of the people of God (verse 5). The faithful are called upon to praise the Lord "upon an instrument of ten strings, and upon the psaltery; upon the harp with a solemn sound" (Psalm 92:3).

Instrumental music was a prominent part of the God ordained dedication of Solomon's temple (2 Chronicles 5:13, 14). David regarded singing with instruments as a law of God. "Take a psalm," he said, "and bring hither the timbrel, the pleasant harp with the psaltery. ... For this was a statute for Israel, and a law of the God of Jacob" (Psalm 81:2, 4).

Amos 8:5

"Saying, When will the new moon be gone, that we may sell corn? and the sabbath, that we may set forth wheat, making the ephah small, and the shekel great, and falsifying the balances by deceit?"

Strange as it may seem, this text has been quoted to "prove" that the Sabbath was to come to an end. But the context makes clear that Amos was condemning the hypocritical Israelites, who wished for the Sabbath hours to quickly end so that they could return to their dishonest business dealings. It was a classic example of formal apostates begrudging the time claimed by God in worship and longing for the sun to set, that they might be released from the yoke of a Sabbath they did not spiritually regard.

The new moon refers to the first day of the month when business was suspended and sacrifice offered (1 Samuel 20:5, 24; Numbers 28:11; 2 Kings 4:23). They were always glad to see that day end also, because they had no relish for the spiritual worship prescribed.

Some have made it seem that it is God that is asking the question, "When will the new moon be gone … and the sabbath?" Please notice that it is not God, but the unscrupulous cheaters who longingly ask the question. Those who make this false application claim that God answers His own question in verse 9 where He tells when the Sabbath will come to an end. They apply verse 9 to the darkness over the earth at the crucifixion of Jesus, and mistakenly claim that the Ten Commandments were finished at that time.

Actually, verse 9 has reference to the signs of a final judgment that will be visited on the earth, when the sun will be darkened and the moon not give her light. Isaiah spoke of the same event (Isaiah 13:10; Joel 2:31) as did Jesus (Matthew 24:29) and John the Revelator (Revelation 6:12). It is nowhere connected to the death of Christ or the abolishing of the law of God.

Malachi 4:5, 6

"Behold, I will send you Elijah the prophet before the coming of the great and dreadful day of the LORD: And he shall turn the heart of the fathers to the children, and the heart of the children to their fathers, lest I come and smite the earth with a curse."

Will Elijah be reincarnated before Jesus returns to the earth? Some think so on the basis of this verse. But notice that Jesus in His day commented "That Elias is come already, and they knew him not, but have done unto him whatsoever they listed. … Then the disciples understood that he spake unto them of John the Baptist" (Matthew 17:12, 13).

You may remember that even though Jesus said that John was Elijah, John vehemently denied it. "And they asked him, what then? Art thou Elijah? And he saith, I am not" (John 1:21).

This sounds most perplexing, doesn't it? But now let us read two texts that will explain the riddle. Even before his birth, it was prophesied of John that "Many of the children of Israel shall he turn to the Lord their God. And he shall go before him in the spirit and power of Elijah … to make ready a people for the Lord" (Luke 1:16, 17).

Instead of actually being Elijah, John's work was to be in the "spirit and power" of Elijah. Jesus completed the clarification when he said concerning John's ministry: "And if ye will receive it, this is Elijah, which was for to come" (Matthew 11:14). This makes it abundantly clear that John's message was the Elijah message for his day. It was given in the spirit, power, and boldness of Elijah's call to repentance. Just before Jesus comes, another message of equal power and boldness is to be given to prepare the world for the second coming of Jesus.

Matthew 3:10-12

"And now also the axe is laid unto the root of the trees: therefore every tree which bringeth not forth good fruit is hewn down, and cast into the fire. I indeed baptize you with water unto repentance: but he that cometh after me is mightier than I, whose shoes I am not worthy to bear. he shall baptize you with the Holy Ghost, and with fire: Whose fan is in his hand, and he will thoroughly purge his floor, and gather his wheat into the garner; but he will burn up the chaff with unquenchable fire."

Please notice that "fire" is mentioned in all three verses. In verse 10, the reference is unmistakably to the punishment of the wicked in the fires of destruction. In verse 12 there is even less question: the fire refers to the "unquenchable" fire of hell. Then what about verse 11, the verse in between? It certainly would not switch the line of thought. Christ is pictured as One who will reward the righteous with the mighty power of the Spirit, and punish the wicked with the consuming fire described in the verses before and after. Both the Old and New Testaments speak of God as a "consuming fire" (Deuteronomy 4:24; Hebrews 12:29).

Just as convincing also is the fact that all three of the verses clearly portray two classes—the good and the bad, the saved and the lost. In verse 10 it's the good tree and the bad, with the bad being "cast into the fire." In verse 12 it is the wheat and the chaff, and the chaff "will burn up." The verse in between—verse 11—describes the two groups as those who are baptized with the Holy Ghost and those who are baptized with fire. Sin will either be burned out now by the Holy Spirit or burned up then by His consuming presence. "He is like a refiner's fire … and he shall purify the sons of Levi" (Malachi 3:2, 3). Those who refuse to be purified from sin now will be burned up, with the sin, in the unquenchable fire.

Matthew 5:17

"Think not that I am come to destroy the law, or the prophets: Iam not come to destroy, but to fulfil"

It is quite evident from the opening words of this text that Christ was reading the minds of His critics who were accusing Him of doing away with the law. He said, *"Think not* that I am come to destroy the law or the prophets: I am not come to destroy, but to fulfil." Instead of abolishing it, He was actually doing the opposite. The word "fulfil" means literally "to fill; to make full." The same word is used in Matthew 3:15 where Jesus spoke concerning His baptism: "Suffer it to be so now: for thus it becometh us to fulfil all righteousness."

There is nothing in the word which signifies "to bring an end to" or "abolish." The law and prophets included not just the Ten Commandments, but all the Old Testament writings. Christ fulfilled those Scriptures, just as He fulfilled all righteousness at His baptism, by obedience to them. Paul used the word in Colossians 1:25: "Whereof I am made a minister, … to fulfil the word of God." This does not mean to bring the word of God to an end, but rather to fully carry it out in obedience. In Romans 8:4, the sense is clearly revealed by the same word used in this sentence: "That the righteousness of the law might be fulfilled in us, who walk not after the flesh, but after the Spirit." Even those who seek to abolish the law must admit that the righteousness of those who walk after the Spirit is not "fulfilled" by being abolished. Yet this is the same word used in Matthew 5:17 to "fulfil" the law.

Finally, Paul gives a classic example of the word "fulfil" in Galatians 6:2: "Bear ye one another's burdens and so fulfil the law of Christ." Not one Christian believes that the law of Christ has been abolished. Neither should any Christian feel that the "law and the prophets" have been abolished. Romans 13:8-10 tells how to fulfil the law of the Ten Commandments by obedience to it.

Matthew 5:19

"Whosoever therefore shall break one of these least commandments, and shall teach men so, he shall be called the least in the kingdom of heaven: but whosoever shall do and teach them, the same shall be called great in the kingdom of heaven."

This text does not mean that men who break God's commandments will get to heaven, even though in a minor position. Jesus was clearly stating the attitude that the kingdom will take toward those who break the least commandment, or teach others to do so. They will be counted totally unworthy of salvation. They are considered the very lowest of the low by heavenly beings. Verse 20 enlarges on the fate of such people in the most emphatic terms: They "shall in no case enter into the kingdom of heaven."

Matthew 10:28

"And fear not them which kill the body, but are not able to kill the soul: but rather fear him which is able to destroy both soul and body in hell."

Jesus clearly teaches in this text that the soul is not naturally immortal. It can and will be destroyed in hell. But what does He mean about killing the body, but not the soul? Is it possible for the soul to exist apart from the body? Some say it is, but the Bible indicates otherwise.

The Greek word "psuche" has been translated "soul" in this text, but in 40 other texts it has been translated "life." For example, Jesus said, "Whosoever will lose his life (psuche) for my sake shall find it" (Matthew 16:25).

But what of Matthew 10:28? Put in the word "life" instead of "soul" and the text makes perfect sense in its consistency with the rest of the Bible. The contrast is between one who can take the physical life and Him who can take away eternal life. Proof lies in the words of Jesus: "And I say unto you my friends, Be not afraid of them that kill the body, and after that have no more that they can do. But I will forewarn you whom ye shall fear: Fear him, which after he hath killed hath power to cast into hell" (Luke 12:4, 5).

In other words, the word "soul" here means not only life, but eternal life. Notice that Luke says everything just like Matthew except that he does not say "kills the soul." Instead he says "cast into hell." They mean the same thing. Men can only kill the body and take away the physical life. God will cast into hell and take away eternal life. Not only will their bodies be destroyed in that fire, but their lives will be snuffed out for all eternity.

Matthew 15:11

"Not that which goeth into the mouth defileth a man; but that which cometh out of the mouth, this defileth a man."

As a setting for this text, begin reading from verse 2. The Jews had a tradition requiring that the hands should be ceremonially washed after each contact with a Gentile. They chided Jesus and His disciples for not following the custom. Christ responded with the words of verse 11: "Not that which goeth into the mouth defileth a man; but that which cometh out of the mouth, this defileth a man."

In verse 15, Peter said to Jesus, "Declare unto us this parable." Please notice that this is a parable and should not be literally applied. In fact, Jesus explained the parable so that we need not speculate about the meaning. He concluded His explanation with these words, "For out of the heart proceed evil thoughts, murders, adulteries, fornications, thefts, false witness, blasphemies: These are the things which defile a man: but to eat with unwashen hands defileth not a man" (verses 19, 20).

Get the picture? The Jewish leaders were upset about the custom of ceremonial washing of hands, while at the same time, they had murder in their hearts toward Christ. Jesus was exposing the absurdity of their posture. The ceremonial uncleanness was only an imagined defilement. The evil thoughts were true defilement. The question of diet was not involved at all. There was no eating or drinking at the heart of the issue. It was ceremonial washing of the hands versus murder in the heart. One defiled, and the other did not.

Matthew 16:18

"And I say also unto thee, That thou art Peter, and upon this rock I will build my church; and the gates of hell shall not prevail against it."

Immediately after Peter's great confession of Christ as the Son of God, Jesus spoke the words of this text, "Thou art Peter" and Jesus used the same Greek word that is used 161 times in the New Testament for Simon Peter—"Petros." In fact, the word "Petros" is never used for any other purpose in the New Testament than to designate Peter. The name means "pebble" or "rolling stone."

But then after Jesus called Peter by his name Petros, He said, "Upon this rock I will build my church." And this time Christ used the word "petra" for "rock." The word "petra" denotes a huge, unmoving boulder—a veritable Gibraltar. This word is never used to designate Peter. Instead it is used repeatedly to describe Jesus Himself, as in 1 Corinthians 10:4. In other words, the church was not built upon the unstable Peter (Petros), who had to be rebuked by Christ as Satan's agent in verse 23, but upon Christ (petra), the Rock of Salvation. Peter's confession of Jesus as the Son of God constituted a firm rock of truth also, but the shifting character of the unconverted Peter was not designated by Jesus as the church's foundation.

Please notice that, after Peter's confession, "Thou art the Christ, the Son of the living God," Jesus assured Peter, "You're right, and this was revealed to you from above. And I'm telling you, Peter, that on this foundation (or rock) I will found my church." It was that confessed truth of Christ's divinity which has been the Gibraltar base for the church through the ages.

Matthew 16:19
(See my comments on John 20:23)

Matthew 16:28

"Verily I say unto you, There be some standing here, which shall not taste of death, till they see the Son of man coming in his kingdom."

This verse can be understood only in the light of what immediately followed—the transfiguration. The very next verse describes that experience and how God spoke out of the cloud saying, "This is my beloved Son, in whom I am well pleased" (Matthew 17:5).

How did the appearance of Moses and Elijah relate to the coming of Jesus? And how can we know that Christ's words in Matthew 16:28 were referring to that event? The answer is in 2 Peter 1:16-18: "For we have not followed cunningly devised fables, when we made known unto you the power and *coming of our Lord Jesus Christ*. For he received from God the Father honor and glory, when there came such a voice to him from the excellent glory, This is my beloved Son, in whom I am well pleased. And this voice which came from heaven we heard, when we were with him in the holy mount."

Please take note that this transfiguration experience, recorded by Peter, is described as the "coming of our Lord Jesus Christ." Why? Because Moses and Elijah appeared with Him on the mount. One of them was translated without seeing death, and the other experienced a special resurrection. Thus they represent all who will be saved at the second coming of Christ. Moses symbolized the saints who will be raised to eternal life at that time, and Elijah represented those who will be translated without seeing death.

Moses' resurrection is described in Jude 9, where Michael the archangel is pictured as contending with Satan over the body of Moses. Some have questioned if this experience really establishes the resurrection of Moses. But why else would the angel of the resurrection be by the graveside disputing over a body? Please note 1 Thessalonians 4:16, where the "voice of the archangel" will open the graves of the dead. Clearly the archangel was by Moses' grave for only one purpose—to raise him to life despite Satan's efforts to prevent it.

Matthew 18:18

"Verily I say unto you, Whatsoever ye shall bind on earth shall be bound in heaven: and whatsoever ye shall loose on earth shall be loosed in heaven."

Prior to this text about binding and loosing, Jesus had been talking about the church taking action to disfellowship a member. Inverse 15, Christ advised going alone to the one who has transgressed. If that doesn't work, He said, "Go again and take two or three witnesses." If they won't be reconciled after that, Jesus said take it to the church and "let him be unto thee as an heathen man and a publican."

When the church takes such an action to disfellowship an unworthy member from the body of Christ, Jesus assured that it would be confirmed in heaven. "Whatsoever ye shall bind on earth shall be bound in heaven: and whatsoever ye shall loose on earth shall be loosed in heaven" (verse 18). This was no bestowal of individual power on men, but an assurance of support for His church as it moved in harmony with His word to accept members into His body, and to uphold the highest standards for those members.

Matthew 22:31, 32

"… have ye not read that … I am the God of Abraham, and the God of Isaac, and the God of Jacob? God is not the God of the dead, but of the living."

It is often overlooked that Jesus was talking about the resurrection when He spoke these words. He did not mean that Abraham, Isaac, or Jacob were alive then, but they would be alive in the resurrection because He was the God who could give life to the dead.

Here's the full text which clarifies the matter: "But as touching the resurrection of the dead, have ye not read that which was spoken unto you by God, saying, I am the God of Abraham, and the God of Isaac, and the God of Jacob? God is not the God of the dead, but of the living" (verses 31, 32).

The topic under discussion was the resurrection, not the state of the dead. He alluded to those patriarchs only in their relation to the resurrection—an assurance that they would have a part in it. Romans 4:17 makes it clear that God "quickeneth the dead, and calleth those things which be not as though they were." Don't miss the point that, concerning the raising of the dead, God speaks of their resurrected life as though it were already accomplished.

Matthew 25:46

"And these shall go away into everlasting punishment: but the righteous into life eternal."

It is well to notice that Jesus did not say that the wicked would suffer "everlasting punishing." He said "everlasting punishment." What is the punishment for sin? "Them that know not God … shall be punished with everlasting destruction from the presence of the Lord" (2 Thessalonians 1:9). There it is—plainly spelled out. The punishment is destruction, and it is of eternal duration. In other words, it is a destruction which never ends because there will be no resurrection from that destruction.

Paul says, "The wages of sin is death" (Romans 6:23). John describes that death as "the second death" in Revelation 21:8. That death, or destruction, will be eternal.

Matthew 28:1

"In the end of the sabbath, as it began to dawn toward the first day of the week, came Mary Magdalene and the other Mary to see the sepulcher."

Some modern religionists contend, on the basis of this text, that the resurrection took place late Sabbath afternoon. They interpret the "end of the Sabbath" as drawing near its close, and "dawning toward the first day of the week" as approaching sunset on Saturday night.

This interpretation falls completely apart when we consider the account of Mark in the next gospel. He also describes the same women as they come to the tomb on Sunday morning. No one can deny that it was "very early in the morning the first day of the week … at the rising of the sun" (Mark 16:2).

Some have argued that these same women had been there late Sabbath afternoon and had found the tomb empty and Jesus' body gone. But this could not be. Why? Because Mark records their conversation as they approached the tomb on Sunday morning: "And they said among themselves, who shall roll us away the stone from the door of the sepulcher?" (Mark 16:3).

If they had been there Sabbath afternoon and found the tomb empty, why would they ask for help to roll away the stone 12 hours later? The fact is that Matthew 28:1 is referring to the Sunday morning visit also. The word "dawn," as used in the Bible, invariably refers to the early morning as day breaks. It doesn't "dawn" toward sunset or darkness.

In the light of these facts, we can easily see that the words "in the end of the Sabbath" actually belong to the preceding verse. The translators had to separate the words, sentences, chapters, and verses as well as supply all the punctuation marks. The original inspired manuscript was just one solid line of letters, with no separation between words.

We have seen that the women came on Sunday morning to learn, for the first time, about the empty tomb. But something was done late Sabbath afternoon, in the end of the Sabbath. It is described in the preceding verse, Matthew 27:66: "So they went, and made the sepulcher sure, sealing the stone, and setting a watch." How do we know when this sealing took place? Verses 62-64 tell us clearly: "Now the next day, that followed the day of preparation, the chief priests and Pharisees came together unto Pilate, Saying … Command therefore that the sepulcher be made sure until the third day, lest his disciples come by night, and steal him away."

This proves that the sealing took place on the Sabbath, following Friday, the preparation day. It also took place just before dark because the expressed fear was that the disciples might "come by night" and steal the body. So they hastened to set up their watch to guard the tomb as night approached.

Now we can perfectly understand the two verses with the proper division of the sentences: "So they went, and made the sepulcher sure, sealing the stone, and setting a watch in the end of the sabbath. As it began to dawn toward the first day of the week, came Mary Magdalene and the other Mary to see the sepulcher."

Mark 4:11, 12

"And he said unto them, Unto you it is given to know the mystery of the kingdom of God. but unto them that are without, all these things are done in parables: That seeing they may see, and not perceive; and hearing they may hear, and not understand; lest at any time they should be converted, and their sins should be forgiven them."

The question raised here is whether Christ used parables to deliberately frustrate a certain class in their desire to be converted. Revelation 22:17 makes it plain that "whosoever will" may come and be accepted into the kingdom. "The Lord is … longsuffering to us-ward, not willing that any should perish, but that all should come to repentance" (2 Peter 3:9). Obviously there is no intention of Christ to hide any truth that would lead a soul to repentance and conversion.

The meaning is clarified completely when we read the parallel account in Matthew's gospel. He gives the reason why they hear not and see not. "For this people's heart is waxed gross, and their ears are dull of hearing, and their eyes they have closed; lest at any time they should see with their eyes, and hear with their ears, and should understand with their heart, and should be converted, and I should heal them" (Matthew 13:15). Thus the arbitrary act of seeing is not on God's part, but theirs. Zechariah declared, "Yea, they made their hearts as an adamant stone, lest they should hear the law ..." (Zechariah 7:12).

Mark 9:43, 44

"And if thy hand offend thee, cut if off: it is better for thee to enter into life maimed, than having two hands to go into hell, into the fire that never shall be quenched: Where their worm dieth not, and the fire is not quenched."

In this verse the word "hell" is translated from the Greek word "gehenna," which is another name for the valley of Hinnom located just outside the walls of Jerusalem. There the refuse and bodies of animals were cast into an ever-smoldering fire to be consumed. What might escape the flames was constantly being destroyed by maggots which fed on the dead bodies. Gehenna symbolized a place of total destruction.

Jesus taught in this verse that the fires of hell could not be quenched or put out by anyone. Isaiah said, "They shall not deliver themselves from the power of the flame" (Isaiah 47:14). Yet he hastened to say in the same verse that "there shall not be a coal to warm at, nor fire to sit before it." So the unquenchable fire will go out after it has consumed the wicked as stubble. Jerusalem burned with unquenchable fire according to Jeremiah 17:27 when it was totally destroyed (2 Chronicles 36:19).

The flames and worms of "gehenna" represented the total annihilation and obliteration of sin and sinners. Earlier apostasy and idol worship in the valley of Hinnom (Jeremiah 32:35), and God's judgments on Israel as a consequence, marked it as a symbol of punishment and judgment. God warned in Jeremiah 7:31-33 that it would become the "valley of slaughter" where the "carcases of this people shall be meat for the fowls of the heaven." With the fires of "gehenna" burning before their eyes, Jesus could not have spoken a more graphic word to the Pharisees to describe the final, total destruction of sinners.

Those who cite this text to support their doctrine of the natural immortality of the soul are thrown into a real dilemma. Why? Because the fire and worms are working not upon disembodied souls, but *bodies*! According to Jesus, those who are cast into the lake of fire will go in bodily form, and this text confirms that truth. The verses before and after this text speak of the hands, feet, and bodies of those who suffer the Gehenna fire. In Matthew 5:30 Christ said, "the whole body" would be cast into hell.

In Isaiah 66:24, the same "gehenna" picture of hell is presented with the unquenchable flame and the destroying worms. But in this case the word "carcases" is used, revealing the fact that the fire consumes dead bodies, not disembodied souls. Speaking of the enemies of the Lord, Isaiah 51:8 says that "the worm shall eat them like wool"—a picture of being put out of existence.

Luke 9:60

"Jesus said unto him, Let the dead bury their dead: but go thou and preach the kingdom of God."

This verse reveals one man's response to Christ's call of discipleship. From the context of this passage, it seems quite apparent that the man's father was not yet dead. If the father had been dead, the son would have had no opportunity to accompany Christ and the disciples. In that hot country, with no embalming, bodies had to be buried immediately. The man was asking to postpone following the Lord until his father had passed away and been buried.

Christ's answer exposed the procrastinator. It indicated the high priority of obedience. Nothing must stand in the way of instant response to the call of Jesus. The Bible speaks of a certain sinner being "dead while she liveth" (1 Timothy 5:6).

In Luke 9:60, Jesus was rebuking the man with these words: "Let the (spiritually) dead bury their (physically) dead: but go thou and preach the kingdom of God." In other words, make your decision while the call is strong and the conviction of truth is urgent. Delay could result in discouragement and loss of interest.

Luke 15:22

"But the father said to his servants, Bring forth the best robe, and put it on him; and put a ring on his hand, and shoes on his feet."

Some have used this Scripture to justify the wearing of jewelry, but remember that this story is a parable and all the characters and events are symbolic of spiritual realities. God is represented by the father in the story, and the children could be any of us who profess to be in His family.

Primarily the love and compassion of God is portrayed in dealing with the backslider. His willingness to forgive and accept the repentant prodigal stands out as the major theme. All the actions of the father toward the returning son represent specific attitudes of God in restoring those who seek forgiveness.

The placing of the father's coat around his son's rags symbolizes the imputed righteousness of God, which must cover our miserable sins and failures. The sign of servitude was removed when the father commanded that shoes be placed on his feet—an act signifying acceptance into the rights of sonship. Then, finally, the signet ring was placed on the prodigal's finger to represent the restoration to full authority in conducting the family business interests. Such rings were not worn as ornaments, but for the practical necessities of signing official documents and discharging legal obligations (Esther 3:10; 8:2). To use this parabolic incident to defend modern ornamentation is totally unreasonable and unbiblical.

Luke 16:16

"The law and the prophets were until John: since that time the kingdom of God is preached, and every man presseth into it."

The "law and the prophets" refers to all the writings of the Old Testament. Some who take a superficial view of this text conclude that the whole body of Old Testament Scriptures lost their authority when John began to preach. Nothing could be farther from the truth. Jesus was merely stating that before John's ministry, the "law and the prophets" were all that men had. They constituted man's primary guide to salvation.

Was Jesus implying that those ancient Scriptures would end when the gospel began to be proclaimed? Not at all. The word "until" is used in other passages to show continuing force and application. Refer to Matthew 28:15 and Romans 5:13, where the same Greek word "mechri" is used.

Jesus emphatically affirmed the authority of the Old Testament scriptures, declaring that not a "jot" or "tittle" would be removed. In truth the only Bible available to the first generation New Testament church was the writings of the Old Testament. Believers found their strongest confirmation of faith in it. On one occasion Jesus set forth those writings as sufficient to guide men to heaven (Luke 16:29-31) Paul repeatedly appealed to the law and the prophets in support of his message (Acts 26:22; 28:23).

"Since that time" refers to the time since John began to preach, when additional light had been shining on the pathway of salvation. That new revelation of truth, especially through Christ and His teachings, had brought huge crowds into the way of light and truth. Jesus described it as "every man presseth into it."

Luke 16:22, 23

"And it came to pass, that the beggar died, and was carried by the angels into Abraham's bosom: the rich man also died, and was buried; And in hell he lift up his eyes, being in torments, and seeth Abraham afar off and Lazarus in his bosom."

Either this story about the rich man and Lazarus is literally true or it is a parable. Here are four reasons why it could not possibly be literalistic:

1. The beggar died and was taken by the angels to Abraham's bosom. No one believes that Abraham's literal bosom is the abode of the righteous dead. It is a figurative or parabolic expression. Incidentally, the angels will gather the saints, but according to Matthew 24:30, 31, this will take place at the coming of Jesus, not at a person's death.

2. Heaven and hell were separated by a gulf, and yet the persons in each could converse with each other. There are probably few individuals in the world who believe that this will be literally true of the saved and the lost (Luke 16:26).

3. The rich man was in hell with a body. He had eyes, a tongue, etc. (Luke 16:24). How did his body get into hellfire instead of into the grave? I know of no one who teaches that the bodies of the wicked go into hell as soon as they die. This story could not be literal.

4. The request for Lazarus to dip the tip of his finger in water and come through the flames to cool the rich man's tongue is obviously not literal. How much moisture would be left and how much relief would it give? The whole story is unrealistic and parabolic.

The rich man undoubtedly represented the Jews in the parable because only a Jew would pray to "father Abraham." The beggar symbolized the Gentiles, who were counted unworthy to receive the truth. In Matthew 15:27, the Canaanite woman acknowledged that her people were beggars at the table of the Jews.

Christ probably chose the name of Lazarus to use in the parable because later he would actually raise Lazarus from the dead. And the climactic point of the entire parable is found in verse 31: "If they hear not Moses and the prophets, neither will they be persuaded, though one rose from the dead." Sure enough, they didn't believe even when one named Lazarus was raised before them.

Luke 17:34-36

"I tell you, in that night there shall be two men in one bed; the one shall be taken, and the other shall be left. Two women shall be grinding together; the one shall be taken, and the other left. Two men shall be in the field; the one shall be taken, and the other left."

Secret rapture advocates take this text as evidence of a secret coming of Christ to snatch away His saints. But to get the whole picture, begin reading in verse 26. Jesus described Noah's day and Lot's day and said: "Even thus shall it be in the day when the Son of man is revealed" (verse 30). Then He added, "I tell you, in that night there shall be two men in one bed; the one shall be taken, and the other shall be left. …"

How was it in the days of Noah and Lot? Some were taken and some were left. Those taken were taken to safety, and those left were left dead. Jesus said, "This is the way it will be when I come. Some will be taken and some will be left." In fact, verses 36 and 37 make it very plain what Jesus meant: "Two men shall be in the field; the one shall be taken, and the other left. And they answered and said unto him, Where, Lord? And he said unto them, Wheresoever the body is, thither will the eagles be gathered together."

The disciples wanted to know where the others would be left, and Christ asserted they would be left dead. In one other text Jesus used similar language: "For wheresoever the carcass (dead body) is, there will the eagles be gathered together" (Matthew 24:28). Some may object and say that eagles are not known to gather in flocks and feed on dead bodies, but here's what the Bible says concerning them: "Doth the eagle mount up at thy command, and make her nest on high? … Her young ones also suck up blood: and where the slain are, there is she" (Job 39:27, 30).

The obvious meaning of Christ's words is that, just as in Noah's day and Lot's day, the righteous will be taken to safety and the wicked slain (by the brightness of His coming). The bodies of the wicked will be scattered over the earth for the birds of prey.

There is no secret rapture here. The term is unknown in the Bible, and so is the doctrine.

Luke 23:43

*"And Jesus said unto him, Verily I say unto thee,
Today shalt thou be with me in paradise."*

Some have assumed from this verse that souls go to
their reward immediately after death, a teaching which
goes contrary to scores of other Bible texts. Notice two
things wrong with this assumption. First: Even though
Jesus told the thief, "Verily I say unto thee, Today shalt
thou be with me in paradise," three days later He told
Mary that He had not yet ascended to His Father.
Here is the evidence that His Father was in
Paradise: Revelation 2:7 says the tree of life "is in the
midst of the paradise of God," and Revelation 22:1,2
describes the tree of life by the side of the river of
life which flows, in turn, from the throne of God. So
there is no question about the Father's throne being
located in Paradise. The question is: How could Jesus
have told the thief that He would be with him in
Paradise that day when He did not go there until three
days later?
In the second place, Jesus and the thief did not
even die on the same day. When the soldiers came just
before sunset to take the bodies off the cross, Jesus was
already dead (John 19:32-34). The thieves were very
much alive, and their legs were broken to hasten death
and to prevent them from escaping. They undoubtedly
lived past sunset into the hours of the Sabbath and possibly longer. So how could Jesus assure the thief of being
with Him in Paradise that day when they did not both
die on "that day"?
The apparent contradictions clear up when we consider that the punctuation of Luke 23:43 was added by
uninspired men when our English Bible was translated.
They placed a comma before the word "today," when in
reality it should have been placed after the word "today."
Then the verse would correctly read: "Verily I say unto
thee today, Thou shalt be with me in Paradise." In other
words, Jesus was saying: "I give you the assurance today,
when it seems I can save no man—today, when my
disciples have forsaken me and I'm dying as a criminal
dies, I assure you of salvation."
Please notice that the thief did not ask to be taken
to Paradise then. He asked, "Lord remember me when

thou comest into thy kingdom." That's exactly when he will be remembered and taken into that kingdom.

John 1:17

"For the law was given by Moses, but grace and truth came by Jesus Christ."

John certainly does not mean that no grace or truth existed before Christ came, but that the "fullness" of grace was revealed in Christ. In contrast to the old covenant system reflecting in the law of Moses, the life and ministry of Christ completely overshadowed it. John uses superlative expressions like these to describe the coming of Jesus into the world: "glory," "full of grace and truth" (verse 14), "his fullness," "grace for grace" (verse 16). It was like twilight giving way to noonday brightness.

But take note that grace had been in the world from the beginning. Paul speaks of "grace, which was given us in Christ Jesus before the world began" (2 Timothy 1:9). Jeremiah spoke of "grace in the wilderness" (Jeremiah 31:2). Noah found grace in the eyes of the Lord (Genesis 6:8), and so did many other Old Testament characters. But the fullness of grace appeared in the person of Jesus. The law revealed the will of God, but grace gave the power to keep it. "Where sin abounded (through the law operating to expose it), grace did much more abound" (Romans 5:20).

John 2:3-6

"And when they wanted wine, the mother of Jesus saith unto him, They have no wine. Jesus saith unto her, Woman, what have I to do with thee? mine hour is not yet come. His mother saith unto the servants, Whatsoever he saith unto you, do it. And there were set there six waterpots of stone, after the manner of the purifying of the Jews, containing two or three firkins apiece."

Although the fermented and unfermented wines are translated from the same original word, the biblical context establishes that no alcoholic drink is approved in God's Word.

Jesus certainly would not go contrary to the Old Testament Scriptures which specifically forbade fermented wine. Proverbs 20:1 and Proverbs 23:29-32 indisputably condemn the use of alcoholic beverage. Would Christ disobey the Scriptures? It is unconceivable.

It is true that wine is often approved for use in the Bible, but this is the pure juice of the grape without fermentation. Here is evidence that this kind of wine is a blessing: "Thus saith the LORD, As the new wine is found *in the cluster*, and one saith, Destroy it not; *for a blessing is in it*: so will I do for my servants' sakes, that I may not destroy them all" (Isaiah 65:8). This wine is "in the cluster," or fresh from the grape. It is a blessing, but not the "strong wine," "mixed wine," or alcoholic beverage.

John 3:13

"And no man hath ascended up to heaven, but he that came down from heaven, even the Son of man which is in heaven."

The subject of conversation between Christ and Nicodemus centered in the mysteries of the Holy Spirit and the new birth. Nicodemus professed ignorance concerning the subject of conversion, and Jesus reacted with surprise. Then He said to Nicodemus, "If I have told you earthly things, and ye believe not, how shall ye believe, if I tell you of heavenly things? And no man hath ascended up to heaven, but he that came down from heaven, even the Son of man which is in heaven" (verses 12, 13).

In other words, Nicodemus would have a harder time accepting Christ's words about heavenly things because no man had even been there to come back and report on it. Jesus alone had come from there to testify about those heavenly things, and Nicodemus would have to accept it purely by faith. The question was: Who is qualified to testify of those spiritual, heavenly truths? Jesus said, "... We speak that we do know, and testify that we have seen; and ye receive not our witness. If I have told you earthly things, and ye believe not, how shall ye believe, if I tell you of heavenly things? And no man hath ascended up to heaven" (verses 11-13).

Throughout the chapter we are directed back to the point of His own authority and credentials as a faithful witness of heavenly truth. "He that cometh from above is above all: he that is of the earth is earthly, and speaketh of the earth: he that cometh from heaven is above all. And what he hath seen and heard, that he testifieth; and no man receiveth his testimony. He that hath received his testimony hath set to his seal that God is true. For he whom God hath sent speaketh the words of God: for God giveth not the Spirit by measure unto him" (verses 31-34).

Jesus assured Nicodemus that He was a reliable and true witness of the truth because He came down from heaven with the Father's words. No man could make such a claim, therefore a man could speak only of earthly things. Some have used these verses to support a theory that no one has been, or ever will go to heaven. This could not be true because of texts to the contrary. The saints will certainly be there for 1,000 years before the holy city descends to this earth. Here's the evidence:

1. John 13:36-14:3: Here Jesus promised Peter that, afterward, he would follow Him where He was going. Then Jesus said, "I go to prepare a place for you." All the saints will follow Jesus to that place in the Father's house, when He comes the second time.

2. Matthew 5:12: Jesus promised a "reward in heaven" to those who were persecuted for His sake.

3. 1 Peter 1:4: Peter spoke of the incorruptible inheritance "reserved in heaven for you.

4. Revelation 19:1: The Revelator "heard a great voice of much people in heaven." This group of people in heaven is later identified as the bride of Christ, which is the church (verses 7, 8).

5. Revelation 4:1, 2 and 5:1, 9: These verses clearly describe a multitude in heaven who have been redeemed from the earth.

John 5:24

"Verily, verily, I say unto you, He that heareth my word, and believeth on him that sent me, hath everlasting life, and shall not come into condemnation; but is passed from death unto life."

The Christian receives everlasting life as a gift when he accepts Jesus. "And I give unto them eternal life; and they shall never perish" (John 10:28). "He that hath the Son hath life; and he that hath not the Son of God hath not life" (I John 5:12).

Are these verses talking about temporal life or eternal life? Does accepting Christ save us from the first death or the second death? The answer is obvious. Jesus said, "He that … believeth on him that sent me, hath everlasting life, and … is passed from death unto life" (John 5:24). Please note that this death had to be the second death. Receiving everlasting life did not take away the first death—only the second. Although the scriptures tell us that the apostle Paul had eternal life (2 Timothy 4:7, 8), he still suffered the first death. Paul said, "It is appointed unto men once to die" (Hebrews 9:27). This is true of good or bad, saved or lost.

Please note that the eternal life received when we accept Christ does not save us from the first death, but only from the second. "He that overcometh shall not be hurt of the second death" (Revelation 2:11). Only the wicked will be cast into the lake of fire, which is the second death (Revelation 21:8). Because the Christian has everlasting life through the Son, he will never die. The second death cannot touch him, and he will live for eternity. Dying the first death will not take away that promise of life without end, which is the gift of God.

John 7:39

"(But this spake he of the Spirit, which they that believe on him should receive. for the Holy Ghost was not yet given; because that Jesus was not yet glorified.)"

This does not mean that the Holy Spirit had not operated before Pentecost, but only that He had not been manifested in His fullness. Only after Jesus was glorified at His ascension were the assembled praying, waiting disciples to receive the Holy Spirit according to the promise (Acts 1:8, 9; 2:1-4).

The Holy Spirit had been manifested at the time of Creation (Genesis 1:2) and just before the Flood

(Genesis 6:3). David prayed, "Take not thy holy spirit from me" (Psalm 51:11). The Scriptures record also that "the Spirit of the LORD departed from Saul" (1 Samuel 16:14). But only after tarrying at Pentecost did the disciples receive the promised blessing of the fullness of the Holy Spirit, at the time appointed by Christ.

John 8:51
(*See my comments on John 5.24.*)

John 9:31

"Now we know that God heareth not sinners. but if any man be a worshiper of God, and doeth his will, him he heareth."

If God hears no sinner's prayer, then how can one be saved? It is true that sin separates a soul from God. "If I regard iniquity in my heart, the Lord will not hear me" (Psalm 66:18). But here is one prayer of the sinner that God will always hear: "And the publican … smote upon his breast, saying, God be merciful to me a sinner" (Luke 18:13).

The publican obviously was not trying to hold or "regard" sin in his heart. He wanted deliverance from it. He was earnestly and humbly seeking forgiveness. Such sinners will always be heard and forgiven. Not only was the publican's prayer answered, Jesus said, "… This man went down to his house justified …" (Luke 18:14). He was fully accepted, forgiven, and placed in the family of God.

John 10:28

"And I give unto them eternal life; and they shall never perish, neither shall any man pluck them out of my hand."

Two wonderful assurances are given in this text. God's faithful obedient children have eternal life as a qualitative factor even while waiting for Jesus to come. Secondly, no man is able to take that "eternal life" quality away from them and separate them from the Father.

Let's look at these statements carefully. How can it be said that we have eternal life before Jesus comes to bestow immortality upon us? In John 5:24, Jesus said, "… He that heareth my word, and believeth on him that sent me, hath everlasting life, and shall not come into condemnation; but is passed from death unto life."

The born-again Christian immediately begins to partake of the divine nature of Jesus. Peter describes the faith process as claiming the promises of salvation that "… ye might be partakers of the divine nature" (2 Peter 1:4). As long as this faith relationship continues and God's sheep hear His voice and follow Him, there is a sharing of the very life of Christ. Although no human being can deprive the Christian of that shared eternal life, the Christian can always choose to take himself away from Christ by severing the relationship which provides the divine nature (eternal life). In that case, he removes himself from the Father's hand and severs himself also from the source of everlasting life.

John 11:26

"And whosoever liveth and believeth in me shall never die. Believest thou this?"

Jesus introduced this text with these words, "I am the resurrection, and the life: he that believeth in me, though he were dead, yet shall he live: And whosoever liveth and believeth in me shall never die" (verses 25, 26).

It is quite apparent that Jesus was talking about the second death when he said "shall never die." This person had already lived the first life, died, and lived again in the resurrection. Revelation 2:11 assures that the overcomer "… shall not be hurt of the second death." Although "it is appointed unto men once to die …" (Hebrews 9:27), those who are accepted by Christ shall never die that second eternal death.

John 20:23

"Whosoever sins ye remit, they are remitted unto them: and whosoever sins ye retain, they are retained."

The key to understanding this verse is found in verse 21 of this chapter: "… as my Father hath sent me, even so send I you."

How had the Father sent the Son into the world? To speak His own words? Jesus said, "For I have not spoken of myself; but the Father which sent me, he gave me a commandment, what I should say, and what I should speak" (John 12:49). Again Christ said, "… I do nothing of myself; but as my Father hath taught me, I speak these things" (John 8:28). "… My doctrine is not mine, but his that sent me" (John 7:16). "… I came down from heaven, not to do mine own will, but the will of him that sent me" (John 6:38).

Clearly then, Jesus sent His disciples as the Father had sent Him. They were not to speak their own words, but His. Paul said that he was only an ambassador for Christ. An ambassador does not speak his own words, but the words of the one he represents. Now we will read the entire text of Paul's words to see what Christ's ambassadors will speak for Him: "… God … hath reconciled us to himself by Jesus Christ, and hath given to us the ministry of reconciliation; To wit, that God was in Christ, reconciling the world unto himself, *not imputing their trespasses unto them*; and hath committed unto us *the word of reconciliation*. Now then we are *ambassadors for Christ*, as though God did beseech you by us; we pray you in Christ's *stead*, be ye reconciled to God" (2 Corinthians 5:18-20).

Please notice that, as an ambassador for Christ, one can carry only His Word to the people. And that word of reconciliation which He has given for the people is that their trespasses are not imputed to them. This is the only way anyone can remit sins. He can pass along Christ' sword about forgiveness and assure them of acceptance as they meet the requirements of that word.

Acts 10:13

"And there came a voice to him, Rise, Peter; kill, and eat."

This chapter gives the interesting account of the Gentile Cornelius, who prayed for the truth.

God appeared to him and told him to send men to Joppa and to invite Peter to come and teach him (verses 3-6).

As the servants of Cornelius approached Joppa, Peter fell into a trance on the housetop and saw a sheet let down from heaven. In the sheet were all manner of beasts, creeping things, and fowls—moles, bats, buzzards, etc. A voice invited Peter to eat them, but he said, "Not so, Lord; for I have never eaten any thing that is common or unclean" (verse 14).

Some people contend that Christ cleansed all food when He was on earth, but if so, Peter knew nothing about it. He had spent three and one-half years with the Master and had listened to His instructions. Yet Peter had gathered no intimation that those unclean animals could be eaten. Peter did not know what the vision meant. Verse 17 says, "Now while Peter doubted in himself what this vision which he had seen should mean, behold, the men … stood before the gate." He was pondering it. Again in verse 19, "While Peter thought on the vision, the Spirit said unto him, Behold, three men seek thee."

Apparently, on the way back to Cornelius' house the Lord answered Peter's ponderings and showed him the meaning of his vision. When he entered the house full of Gentile friends, Peter said, "… Ye know how that it is an unlawful thing for a man that is a Jew to keep company, or come unto one of another nation; but God hath showed me that I should not call any *man* common or unclean" (verse 28, emphasis added).

The meaning was now clear. Peter's vision had nothing to do with diet. It was a sign that the gospel was henceforth to be preached to the Gentiles.

Acts 12:15

"And they said unto her, Thou art mad. But she constantly affirmed that it was even so. Then said they, It is his angel."

Some religious sects believe that people become angels after they die. Did these friends of Peter believe he was dead and that he had become an angel? Not if they believed the words of Scripture.

Mark these facts:

1. Angels existed before any human being died (Genesis 3:24), so the existence of angels does not depend on the death of mortals.

2. Angels belong to a different order of created beings (Psalm 8:5).

3. Children have guardian angels assigned to them (Matthew 18:10).

4. Angels witness all we say or do (Ecclesiastes 5:6).

5. They are constantly ministering to the "heirs of salvation" (Hebrews 1:14).

In the text under consideration, Peter's friends were undoubtedly talking about his guardian angel.

Romans 5:13

"For until the law sin was in the world: but sin is not imputed when there is no law."

Some contend that the phrase "until the law" means that the law did not exist between Adam and Sinai. But the balance of the text, coupled with Romans 4:15, proves the opposite. Sin was imputed to Cain for slaying his brother; therefore the law had to be in effect. God upbraided His people for refusing to keep His commandments and laws (Exodus 16:28). He also honored Abraham, who kept His commandments, statutes, and laws (Genesis 26:5).

The meaning then is clear: The law did not exist in written form prior to Sinai. People were punished for breaking any one of the Ten Commandments before Sinai, indicating that the law existed and sin was imputed. Note the Ten Commandments before Sinai:

First	Genesis 35:2-4
Second	Genesis 31:19-34
Third	Genesis 12:3
Fourth	Exodus 16:4-26
Fifth	Genesis 9:20-25
Sixth	Genesis 4:8-15
Seventh	Genesis 39:7-9
Eighth	Genesis 44:8-16
Ninth	Genesis 27:12
Tenth	Genesis 25:29-34; 27:1-45

Israel had largely lost sight of the principles of God's law while in Egyptian bondage. So God wrote that law with His own finger to bring it forcibly back to mind.

Romans 7:4

"Wherefore, my brethren, ye also are become dead to the law by the body of Christ; that ye should be married to another, even to him who is raised from the dead, that we should bring forth fruit unto God."

Paul is here illustrating the changed status of one who is freed from the bondage of sin to be married to Christ. Three principal figures are used in his illustration: a woman, her husband, and the law of marriage (verses 1-3). Which one of these parties dies? Not the law, as some interpret. If so, the whole argument over adultery would be pointless. There could be no adultery without the law containing the prohibition.

No, it was the husband who died, and he symbolized the "old man of sin" who dies at conversion (Romans 6:6). This death to the law of sin (husband—unconverted nature) was brought about through the "body of Christ," by His death. The condemnation of the law (sentence of death) was nullified by the deliverance wrought through Christ. But please notice that Christ's death cancels only the penalty—not the law itself. Peter says He "… bare our sins in His own body …" (1 Peter 2:24). Paul says Christ tasted "… death for every man" (Hebrews 2:9).

Now that the binding power of the law of sin is broken, the individual is free to marry another, even Christ. The law of marriage has not been canceled. We are "crucified with Christ" as Paul says in Galatians 2:20, but the law remains. With the death of the carnal nature, we no longer "… bring forth fruit unto death" (verse 5). The death sentence of the law has been satisfied through the sacrifice of Jesus, and the new marriage to Christ brings forth obedience through love. Finally, in verse 7 Paul emphasizes again the fact that the Ten Commandment law remains to point out sin: "… for I had not known lust, except the law had said, Thou shalt not covet."

Romans 10:4

"For Christ is the end of the law for righteousness to every one that believeth."

Does this text teach that the Ten Commandment law came to an end through the ministry of Christ? By no means. The word "end" is used here in the sense of "end objective" or "goal." The objective of the law is to lead us to Christ.

Please notice how the same word is used in James 5:11: "… Ye have … seen the end of the Lord; that the Lord is very pitiful, and of tender mercy." This doesn't mean the Lord has come to an end. It means that the whole end objective of His life is to show pity and mercy.

Again we read, "Receiving the end of your faith, even the salvation of your souls" (1 Peter 1:9). Here the end objective, or goal, of one's faith is the salvation of his soul. It has nothing to do with faith actually coming to an end. One more example: "Now the end of the commandment is charity" (1 Timothy 1:5). It means that obedience to the commandment will lead one to charity. In the same sense, Christ is the "end of the law" because the law leads people to Christ. The law did not come to an end.

Romans 11:26

"And so all Israel shall be saved: as it is written, There shall come out of Zion the Deliverer, and shall turn away ungodliness from Jacob."

The context of this chapter makes it very plain that Paul was not talking about Israel after the flesh. Who is the Israel who will be saved? Paul had just finished spelling it out in verses 16-25. He described how the Gentiles would be grafted into the olive tree representing the Jewish people. As the Gentiles (represented by the wild olive tree) were grafted in, they began to partake of "the root and fatness" of the Israelites (verse 17). The "natural branches," or Jews (verse 21), were cut off because of unbelief, and believing Gentiles were accepted as spiritual Israel.

In Galatians 3:29, Paul said, "And if ye be Christ's, then are ye Abraham's seed, and heirs according to the promise." The picture grows clearer still as we read Romans 9:6-8. "For they are not all Israel, which are of Israel: Neither, because they are the seed of Abraham, are they all children: ... That is, They which are the children of the flesh, these are not the children of God: but the children of the promise are counted for the seed."

So it is faith that makes one a spiritual Israelite, not the accident of physical birth. It is the new birth that places Jew and Gentile into the spiritual family of God, all of whom will be saved.

Romans 14:14

"I know, and am persuaded by the Lord Jesus, that there is nothing unclean of itself. but to him that esteemeth any thing to be unclean, to him it is unclean."

It is well to consider this entire chapter in its context. Paul was writing about a problem of judging among the apostolic believers. Verses 4, 10, and 13 exhort against the sin of judging one another. And it was true that a serious division existed in that early church. The Gentile Christians were judging the Jewish Christians, and the Jewish Christians were judging the Gentile Christians.

Notice how the previous verse strikes at the very heart of the issue. "Let us not therefore judge one another any more: but judge this rather, that no man put a stumbling block or an occasion to fall in his brother's way" (verse 13).

What was the basis of the problem? Over what were they judging each other? The Gentiles who had come into the church from paganism were offended because the Jewish Christians ate food that had been offered in sacrifice to idols. And the Jewish Christians judged the Gentile church members because they had no regard for the ceremonial days that they still observed from Judaism.

Some of the Gentile converts were so fearful of eating meat offered to idols that they ate only vegetables. Paul spoke of them in verses 1 and 2. The Jewish Christians thought that was ridiculous and apparently made divisive attacks against their fellow Christians. It was so serious that Paul addressed the problem again in 1 Corinthians 8:8-12. There he elaborated at length on the "weak brother" (the Gentile believer) who esteemed the food unfit to be eaten.

What was Paul's counsel to the Jewish members who were judging the Gentile members? He told them not to eat the food offered to idols if they were in the presence of those who thought it to be wrong. Even though they had knowledge that the idol was nothing, he told the Jewish converts: "And through thy knowledge shall the weak brother perish for whom Christ died? But when ye sin so against the brethren, and wound their weak conscience, ye sin against Christ" (1 Corinthians 8:11, 12).

The food offered to idols was not unclean food (Acts 14:13), but was merely esteemed so by the Gentile converts. It was not a moral issue. Neither was the matter of the ceremonial days, which Paul mentioned in Romans 14:5. He told them to stop judging over those issues and to get on with the work. These matters had nothing to do with the moral questions of the seventh-day Sabbath and the forbidden unclean food.

Romans 14:21

"It is good neither to eat flesh, nor to drink wine, nor any thing whereby thy brother stumbleth, or is offended, or is made weak."

The foods referred to in this chapter were not biblically unclean, but were *esteemed* unclean (verse 14) because they had been used in sacrifice to idols (1 Corinthians 8:1, 13). The wine approved by God is described as "wine in the cluster" (Isaiah 65:8), so both meat and wine were clean of themselves. Though Paul concedes that an idol is "nothing in the world" (1 Corinthians 8:4), and therefore food offered to it is not defiled by being offered, many did not view it that way. They felt the food was contaminated and unfit for Christian consumption. For the sake of such objectors who felt that it was unclean, Paul said it was better not to offend their weak conscience (verse 10) by eating it before them.

1 Corinthians 3:13, 14

"Every man's work shall be made manifest: for the day shall declare it, because it shall be revealed by fire; and the fire shall try every man's work of what sort it is. If any man's work abide which he hath built thereupon, he shall receive a reward."

The first thing to note about these verses is that the apostle is not talking about the eternal reward of the Christian, but rather the reward for service rendered in the ministry. The entire chapter is about methods of planting and building in the establishment of believers and churches. Paul describes his approach and also that of his fellow ministers.

So we can immediately discount any idea of pre-destination or of salvation regardless of one's works. It seems quite clear that Paul was describing an actual situation in which some weak pastors or teachers, after bringing people to Christ, had not followed through with sound instructions about the Christian life. As a result, there had not been satisfactory spiritual growth of the converts. Paul spoke of such inferior teaching as poor building material and indicated that it would be destroyed in the fiery test. The literal fires of the last day are not being referred to here, for the fire represents a testing work, and those who pass through it may be saved (verse 15).

Paul is conveying the sobering thought that even though a minister may repent of his poor workman-ship and be saved himself, the results of his faulty work (weak instruction) cannot be changed. Souls could be lost by his poor building material when they faced severe spiritual stress. Nevertheless, the worker could be saved, because at least he laid the proper foundation in presenting Christ as the basis of salvation.

1 Corinthians 5:5

"To deliver such an one unto Satan for the destruction of the flesh, that the spirit may be saved in the day of the Lord Jesus."

The person under consideration had been guilty of unspeakable moral degeneracy (verse 1). Paul's recommendation is to disfellowship the man from the body of Christ. He used words that cannot be misconstrued: "deliver such an one unto Satan," "purge out," "not to company with," and "put away" (verses 5, 7, 9, 13).

Paul used this strong language because the man had chosen to follow Satan. The church was merely recognizing, and finally making official, what the man had openly decided and declared by his conduct. There was no thought to consign him to the devil, but rather to register on a temporary basis that the man preferred Satan's path to the path of Christ.

What did Paul feel might be the result of this drastic action? His hope was for "the destruction of the flesh." Paul's favorite expression for the unconverted was "the flesh." To the Romans he wrote, "They that are in the flesh cannot please God" (Romans 8:8). Perhaps the shock of being expelled from the fellowship of the church would turn the sinner to repentance and cause him to crucify the flesh, thereby destroying the gross works of the flesh that had brought on his condemnation. Thus his spirit could be transformed and spiritualized for the day of the Lord. He could be restored to church fellowship and saved at the coming of Jesus.

1 Corinthians 7:14

"For the unbelieving husband is sanctified by the wife, and the unbelieving wife is sanctified by the husband: else were your children unclean; but now are they holy."

Paul is here giving some brief answers to questions written to him by the Corinthian believers (verse 1). Apparently a new convert was troubled over the matter of having a heathen companion. Would it desecrate the marriage, thus making it better to separate? Also, what about the children? Would they be defiled by the division in the home?

Paul's counsel was not to separate if the unbelieving companion wanted to preserve the home. "For the unbelieving husband is sanctified by the wife, and the unbelieving wife is sanctified by the husband" (verse 14). Obviously Paul did not mean that the heathen companion would be automatically saved by staying with the Christian spouse, but rather that the marriage status was not desecrated by the heathen alliance—it was still a valid union.

Then Paul adds, "Else were your children unclean; but now they are holy." He was clearly saying that if a divorce were granted on the basis of the marriage itself having been improper, then the children would have to be considered illegitimate, or "unclean." But, no, Paul says the union is holy and therefore the children are "holy" in the sense that they are legitimately born.

Some have assumed that only the children of two believing parents can be saved. But Paul is not talking at all about the salvation of the child. The words "holy" and "sanctified" have the same root meaning, and if the child could be saved, then the heathen parent, being "sanctified" by the Christian spouse, would also be saved. The advice is simply this: don't let religious differences break up an already-established family. It does not affect the status of the marriage before God.

1 Corinthians 11:29, 30

"For he that eateth and drinketh unworthily, eateth and drinketh damnation to himself not discerning the Lord's body. For this cause many are weak and sickly among you, and many sleep."

Some interpret these words to mean that healing is a part of the atonement, and that since Jesus bore our sicknesses on the cross we have just as much right to claim healing as to claim forgiveness. But can we expect an answer for healing with the same confidence that we expect salvation in answer to our prayer?

Those who believe that you can and should accept healing as part of the atonement also support their position with Isaiah 53:4: "Surely he hath borne our griefs (diseases), and carried our sorrows (pain) ..." The important question is: When was this prophecy fulfilled? Was it at the cross? The answer is clearly given by Matthew: "When the even was come, they brought unto him many that were possessed with devils: and he cast out the spirits with his word, and healed all that were sick: That it might be fulfilled which was spoken by Isaiah the prophet, saying, Himself took our infirmities, and bare our sicknesses" (Matthew 8:16, 17).

Thus we see that He bore our diseases while He was living in Galilee, not after His death. The most likely meaning of the text in 1 Corinthians 11:29, 30 is that the Corinthians were contributing to their poor health by intemperance and gluttony associated with the love feasts that preceded the Lord's supper.

1 Corinthians 14:34, 35

"Let your women keep silence in the churches: for it is not permitted unto them to speak; but they are commanded to be under obedience, as also saith the law. And if they will learn any thing, let them ask their husbands at home: for it is a shame for women to speak in the church."

Two principles seem to be involved in this counsel of Paul to the Corinthian church. First, there was definitely a violation of the principle of propriety and decency. In verse 33, Paul said, "God is not the author of confusion, but of peace." Again he admonished, "Let all things be done decently and in order" (verse 40).

It is not hard to visualize the situation which brought the rather stern rebuke from Paul in verses 34 and 35. In that early church, the men and women sat in segregated groups on opposite sides of the room. Apparently some of the women were creating considerable disorder by calling across to their husbands, asking for clarification of certain points in the sermon. Paul commanded them to stop bringing in this confusion and to wait and ask their husbands at home about anything that wasn't clear.

Eastern culture dictated that a modest woman be veiled and remain in the background. There was danger that the women in the Christian church might be linked with the shamelessly bold women whose conduct stigmatized the city of Corinth.

The second principle involved in Paul's counsel had to do with the headship of men in both home and church affairs. The man was primarily responsible for leading out in worship. In 1 Timothy 2:12, Paul warned that women were not "… to usurp authority over the man …" Therefore they should assume no position in the church that would frustrate that divine order of things.

Within these two principles of proper decorum and vested authority, women have served most effectively in the work of the church. They have been called by God into prophetic office (Luke 2:36, 37; Judges 4:4; Acts 21:9) and were given recognition by Paul in public and private witnessing roles (1 Corinthians 11:5). The principles of Paul's counsel apply just as strongly today, even though the absence of a Christian woman's veil does not bring reproach on her church, nor is she stereotyped as a clamorous confuser in the congregation.

1 Corinthians 15:29

"Else what shall they do which are baptized for the dead, if the dead rise not at all? why are they then baptized for the dead?"

This is perhaps one of the most puzzling things that Paul wrote in his epistles. One explanation that fits in perfectly with Paul's line of reasoning revolves around the meaning of the word "for." The Greek word is "huper," and the general translation is "in behalf of." But there are exceptions to this meaning. Sometimes the word is used in the sense of "considering" or "in view of."

For example, 2 Thessalonians 1:4 says: "So that we ourselves glory in you in the churches of God for your patience and faith in all your persecutions …" Here Paul is saying, "We glory in you considering (or in view of) your patience and faith." In Romans 15:9—which reads, "And that the Gentiles might glorify God for his mercy …" —it can be translated "considering his mercy."

Please notice now that this same word "huper," which is translated "for," is used both ways in 1 Corinthians 15:29: "Else what shall they do which are baptized for (considering) the dead, if the dead rise not at all? why are they then baptized for (in view of) the dead?"

If we substitute this other meaning of the word "for," the text makes perfect sense. Paul's whole theme in the chapter is the resurrection—its importance and necessity. He is saying, "Why even be baptized if there is no resurrection from the dead?" The very meaning of baptism would be nullified. With no resurrection, the entire symbolism of baptism—death, burial, and resurrection—would be reduced to an empty ritual.

2 Corinthians 3:7, 8

"But if the ministration of death, written and engraven in stones, was glorious, so that the children of Israel could not stedfastly behold the face of Moses for the glory of his countenance; which glory was to be done away: How shall not the ministration of the spirit be rather glorious?"

Here Paul is contrasting the two covenants—the tables of stone versus the tables of the heart, the letter versus the Spirit, the ministration of death versus the ministration of the Spirit, and the ministration of condemnation versus the ministration of righteousness.

Please notice that the Ten Commandment law was not the old covenant and was not done away. It was the ministration or application of the law, not the law itself, that was done away. This was accomplished through Christ when He delivered us from the curse of condemnation and death. The glory of His ministration of righteousness was so much greater than the glory of the law that it outshone and did away with the former glory. On the tables of stone, the literal letter of the law demanded death. There was no grace or life-giving power. That same law, written in the heart through the action of the Spirit, brought grace, pardon, and power to obey. This was the exceeding glory of the ministration of righteousness.

One more point to remember: What was done away? Verse 7 says that the glory "was to be done away" of that ministration of death. The law was not abolished—only its manner of being ministered or applied.

Now it would be ministered by the Spirit on the heart instead of on the stone. But the same law functioned under both old and new covenants.

2 Corinthians 4:16

"For which cause we faint not; but though our outward man perish, yet the inward man is renewed day by day."

Paul is here making a contrast between the physical and the spiritual. Jesus said something very similar when He gently rebuked the disciples, saying, "… the spirit indeed is willing, but the flesh is weak" (Matthew 26:41).

Paul said the outward (physical) man might wear out and perish. The word he used for "perish" means literally "to be corrupted" or decay. The body grows weak and fatigued, but "the inward man is renewed day by day." This inward man is the same as the "inner man"—a term which Paul uses often to describe the mind or heart. In Ephesians 3:16, that inner man is "strengthened by the spirit," and in Romans 7:22, Paul delighted "in the law of God after the inward man."

There is absolutely no indication that Paul ever connected that inward man with a soul that could leave the body. Nowhere is it used to denote an immortal entity or disembodied spirit.

2 Corinthians 5:6-8

"Therefore we are always confident, knowing that, whilst we are at home in the body, we are absent from the Lord: … We are confident, I say, and willing rather to be absent from the body, and to be present with the Lord."

In verses 1-8, Paul is contrasting the present mortal state with the future immortal life in heaven. Notice the expressions he uses for the two conditions:

earthly house . . . . building of God
this tabernacle . . . . house not made with hands
mortality . . . . our house which is from heaven
in the body . . . . absent from the body
absent from the Lord . . . . present with the Lord

Paul speaks of being clothed with "our house which is from heaven" (verse 2). He longs "that mortality might be swallowed up of life" (verse 4). But the key to the entire discourse lies in the description of a third condition. After desiring to be clothed with immortality, Paul states that "being clothed we shall not be found naked" (verse 3). Putting it yet another way, he said, "… not for that we would be unclothed" (verse 4).

Clearly the naked or unclothed state was neither mortality nor immortality, but death and the grave. Paul realized that one did not pass instantly from being clothed with this tabernacle into being clothed with our house from heaven. Death and the grave came in between, and he referred to this as being unclothed and naked.

In another text Paul spelled out exactly when that change from mortality would take place. In 1 Corinthians 15:52, 53, he wrote, "The trumpet shall sound, … and this mortal must put on immortality." That will be when Jesus comes.

2 Corinthians 12:2, 3

"I knew a man in Christ above fourteen years ago, (whether in the body, I cannot tell; or whether out of the body, I cannot tell: God knoweth;) such an one caught up to the third heaven. And I knew such a man, (whether in the body, or out of the body, I cannot tell: God knoweth;)"

Although this text has been used to "prove" the doctrine of an immortal soul, it has no such connotation at all. It is conceded by practically all commentators that Paul was describing his own experience, because he spoke in the context of his own revelations. He was concerned that no one think he was glorying or boasting about his visions. For this reason, probably, he ascribed the experience to a man he knew.

Paul's soul did not leave his body, in spite of claims to the contrary. If so, he would have been dead, and nowhere does he make any allusion to his death or resurrection.

Paul is speaking of "visions" and "revelations" in the text. He was not puzzled over whether he had died or not. He was merely uncertain as to how he was able to see paradise in that vision. Although it seemed that he was bodily taken to heaven, yet he felt it possible that he was taken there only spiritually. He confessed to complete ignorance as to what actually happened. The physical impressions seemed as though He were "out of the body," in a way of speaking. In the same manner of speech, Paul wrote to the Colossian church, "For though I be absent in the flesh, yet am I with you in the spirit" (Colossians 2:5). No one interprets this to mean that some immortal soul left Paul's body to be with his friends.

The fact is, as Paul said, that only God knows the nature of that spiritual visit to paradise. So we would do well not to base any doctrine on a text that is understood by God only.

Galatians 2:19

"For I through the law am dead to the law, that I might live unto God."

How did Paul become dead to the law through the law?

1. The law pointed out his sin (Romans 3:20).

2. It made sin "exceeding sinful" (Romans 7:13).

3. The law pointed him to Christ (Romans 8:3).

4. Christ gave power to obey the law (Romans 8:4).

5. In Christ he was no longer under the law, but under grace (Romans 6:14).

6. To be under the law means to be guilty of breaking it (Romans 3:19).

7. Through accepting the death of Jesus he was dead to the law because he was no longer breaking it, and it did not condemn him (Romans 7:4).

Galatians 3:19

"Wherefore then serveth the law? It was added because of transgressions, till the seed should come to whom the promise was made; and it was ordained by angels in the hand of a mediator."

The question is often asked: To which law is Paul referring? The answer appears as we consider the sole subject of this chapter. Paul is contrasting condemnation and justification, and the chief point of his argument is that "no man is justified by the law in the sight of God" (verse 11). Please take note that the argument is not whether the law operates or not, but whether it operates as a *justifier* of guilty sinners. Paul clearly spells out in many other texts that the law is necessary as a *revealer* of sin (Romans 3:20; 7:7), but not as a *justifier* from sin.

In verse 18 (the verse just preceding the one under consideration), Paul emphasizes again that the inheritance is not by law, but by promise. And in verse 21 he says, "... if there had been a law given which could have given life, verily righteousness should have been by the law."

These verses make it very clear that Paul is talking about both moral and ceremonial laws in verse 19. Neither of them could save or justify the transgressor. All they could do was condemn the sinner and point forward to "the seed" who "should come." That seed was Christ, and He would be able to justify and deliver them from the condemnation of the law. But even then, the law would not cease to exist. Its function of pointing out sin would ever be needed to turn back to Christ anyone who deviated from the path of justification and obedience.

Galatians 3:23-25

"But before faith came, we were kept under the law, shut up unto the faith which should afterwards be revealed. Wherefore the law was our schoolmaster to bring us unto Christ, that we might be justfied by faith. But after that faith is come, we are no longer under a schoolmaster."

The key to this text is in the first four words: "But before faith came." Paul is talking about his condition of condemnation before he exercised faith in Christ. Being "under the law" is defined in Romans 3:19 as being "guilty before God" and under the sentence of death. During those years of sin Paul was "kept under the law"—held in the prison house of disobedience. In Romans 7:23, he spoke of that experience of condemnation as "… bringing me into captivity to the law of sin."

But even when Paul was outside of Christ, without faith, the law was operating on his conscience, magnifying his misery and condemnation (Romans 7:13) and leading him step by step, like a schoolmaster, to the Saviour. After being directed to Christ by the law, Paul says we are "justified by faith." This is what the law could not do. It could not justify; it could only condemn. Christ freely forgives *and* delivers.

The last point Paul makes is that we are no longer under the law, but under grace. After bringing us to Christ, the law no longer condemns because we, as Christians, do not break it. It will still be there to shepherd us back to Christ if we depart from His grace, but it no longer condemns us as transgressors so long as we abide in Him.

Galatians 4:8-10

"Howbeit then, when ye knew not God, ye did service unto them which by nature are no gods. But now, after that ye have known God, or rather are known of God, how turn ye again to the weak and beggarly elements, whereunto ye desire again to be in bondage? Ye observe days, and months, and times, and years."

The Galatian believers, who had formerly been pagans addicted to ritualistic worship, were being seduced by Jewish converts in the church to revert to a ceremonial, legalistic form of religion in place of knowing and obeying Christ from the heart.

These perverters of the truth were seeking to inculcate the ceremonial law at the church in Galatia. This ceremonial law—epitomized by circumcision (Galatians 5:2, 3, 6, 11; 6:15) and daily, monthly, and yearly observances—was prescribed by God in the law of Moses "until the time of reformation" (Hebrews 9:10), or the death of Christ on the cross (Hebrews 9:8-12).

By compelling the Galatian converts to keep these obsolete laws, the Jewish Christians were effectually eclipsing Christ and His atoning work. They were utterly missing the fact that with His death on the cross, the Messiah would "cause the sacrifice and oblation (the ceremonial law, which foreshadowed the cross) to cease" (Daniel 9:27; See also Matthew 27:50, 51). To practice the ceremonial law after Christ's death on Calvary was a virtual denial of His Messiahship and a betrayal of utter blindness to the significance of that law.

Galatians 4:22-24

"For it is written, that Abraham had two sons, the one by a bondmaid, the other by a freewoman. But he who was of the bondwoman was born after the flesh; but he of the freewoman was by promise. Which things are an allegory: for these are the two covenants; the one from the mount Sinai, which gendereth to bondage, which is Hagar."

Here Paul likens Isaac's birth to the new-covenant relationship, and Ishmael is compared to the old covenant. How do the covenants relate to these two sons of Abraham?

God told Abraham he would have a son by Sarah. Because Sarah was past age, Abraham did not believe it possible for the promise to be fulfilled. So, falling back on the old-covenant principle of trying to do it in human strength and devising, Abraham took a concubine, Hagar, to help things along. The son born of this arrangement was likened to the old-covenant idea of "we will do."

When Isaac was born of Sarah, it was a miracle of grace. God actually brought supernatural life into a dead womb so that Isaac could be born. This represents the regenerating miracle of grace that makes obedience possible under the new covenant. It does not depend on poor promises of man, but on the unfailing assurance of God. "... I will put my laws into their mind, and write them in their hearts: and I will be to them a God, ..." (Hebrews 8:10). Only by the indwelling miracle grace of God can the law be kept.

One fact appears in this allegory of the two covenants. The child of promise represents the new covenant because Abraham obeyed God and followed His instruction in begetting that miracle child. Those under the new covenant are those who obey God's commandments. Ishmael represents disobedience to God's way. Commandment-breakers are the ones who are operating under the old covenant.

Ephesians 2:15
(*See my comments on Colossians 2:14-17*)

Philippians 1:23

"For I am in a strait betwixt two, having a desire to depart, and to be with Christ; which is far better:"

Paul does not say in this text that he will go to be with Christ when he dies. He undoubtedly was using the word "depart" in reference to his death. But the Bible clearly reveals that Paul did not believe his "departure" would mean immediate entrance into heaven. Here's the proof: "... the time of my departure is at hand. I have fought a good fight, I have finished my course, I have kept the faith: *Henceforth* there is laid up for me a crown of righteousness, which the Lord, the righteous judge, shall give me *at that day*; and not to me only, but unto all them also that *love his appearing*" (2 Timothy 4:6-8).

Since Paul obviously did not expect to get his eternal crown at his departure in death, when was it that he anticipated actually being with Christ? "For the Lord himself shall descend from heaven … and so shall we ever be with the Lord" (1 Thessalonians 4:16, 17). There it is. Paul's desire to depart and be with Christ involved the resurrection that would take place at the end of the world. Since the unconscious sleep of death is like a moment, Paul speaks of death and the coming of Christ as almost simultaneous. And so it will seem to those who depart and awake from death to see Jesus coming.

Colossians 2:14-17

"Blotting out the handwriting of ordinances that was against us, which was contrary to us, and took it out of the way, nailing it to his cross; And having spoiled principalities and powers, he made a show of them openly, triumphing over them in it. Let no man therefore judge you in meat, or in drink, or in respect of an holyday, or of the new moon, or of the sabbath days: Which are a shadow of things to come, but the body is of Christ."

A certain law of ordinances was nailed to the cross. This was the ceremonial law of types and shadows that pointed forward to the death of Jesus and that had no further meaning beyond the cross. This is why Paul said it was contrary to the Christian. The rent veil in the temple at the death of Christ (Matthew 27:51) indicated the end of that ordinance of animal sacrifices, and Ephesians 2:15 says that Jesus "… abolished … the law of commandments contained in ordinances."

This is why Paul wrote in Colossians 2:16,17 that we are no longer judged by the meat offerings, drink offerings, and sabbath days "… which are a shadow of things to come …" Take note that these are yearly and not the weekly Sabbath of the moral law. These shadowy sabbaths are described in Leviticus 23:24-37. They fell on certain set days of the month—a different day of the week each year, yet they were called sabbaths. But please observe in verses 37 and 38 how they were distinguished from the weekly Sabbath: "These are the feasts of the Lord, which ye shall proclaim to be holy convocations, to offer an offering made by fire unto the Lord, a burnt offering, and a meat offering, a sacrifice and drink offerings, every thing upon his day, *beside the sabbaths of the Lord …*"

Now the mystery of Colossians 2:16 is completely cleared up. The law of the yearly sabbaths, with all its meat and drink offerings, was nailed to the cross, but the great Ten Commandment law with its weekly Sabbath was not affected by that "blotting out" of ordinances.

1 Thessalonians 3:13

"To the end he may stablish your hearts unblameable in holiness before God, even our Father, at the coming of our Lord Jesus Christ with all his saints."

Does this text teach that all the righteous dead will return with Christ at the end of the world? Who are these "saints" who will attend our Lord at His coming? By allowing the Bible to explain itself, every question is answered. Jesus described those who would come with Him in these words: "When the Son of man shall come in his glory, and all the holy angels with him, then shall he sit upon the throne of his glory" (Matthew 25:31).

Please notice that Jesus said "all the holy angels with him" instead of "with all his saints," as Paul described it in this verse. Is there a contradiction? No. There is perfect harmony when we put all the texts together. Angels are actually called "saints" in the Bible. Moses described the giving of God's law on Mt. Sinai in Deuteronomy 33:2: "The Lord came from Sinai, and rose up from Seir unto them; he shined forth from mount Paran, and he came with ten thousands of saints: from his right hand went a fiery law for them."

Now compare these verses with Psalm 68:17: "The chariots of God are twenty thousand, even thousands of angels: the LORD is among them, as in Sinai, in the holyplace." Here the thousands who attended God at Sinai are identified as angels, although they are called "saints" in Deuteronomy. In the same way, the saints who come with Jesus in 1 Thessalonians 3:13 are identified as angels by the Master Himself in Matthew 25:31.

1 Thessalonians 4:14

"For if we believe that Jesus died and rose again, even so them also which sleep in Jesus will God bring with him."

The first reading of this verse seems to teach that the righteous dead "which sleep in Jesus" will come with Christ when He returns to this earth. But the next three verses make it clear that this could not possibly be the case. Why? Because the "dead in Christ" are raised from their graves when "the Lord himself shall descend from heaven" (verse 16). So it would be impossible for them to come with Christ when He comes to resurrect them.

The true meaning of the verse is revealed when we read 1 Corinthians 15:20, 23: "But now is Christ risen from the dead, and become the firstfruits of them that slept." "But every man in his own order: Christ the firstfruits; afterward they that are Christ's at his coming." Paul stated that Jesus was raised first as a guarantee that the righteous dead would be raised "at his coming." Jesus said, "Because I live, ye shall live also" (John 14:19). His resurrection makes it possible for God to raise us as He did Christ.

And this is exactly what Paul says in 1 Thessalonians 4:14: "For if we believe that Jesus died and rose again, even so them also which sleep in Jesus will God bring (from the dead) with him (Jesus)." The words "with him" do not mean that the resurrected ones will be brought from heaven with Him at His coming, but that God will "bring" up those who will be sleeping in their graves just as He brought Jesus forth from the grave. In Hebrews 13:20, we read that "God … brought again from the dead our Lord Jesus." The text in 1 Thessalonians 4:14 says that God *will bring* those who "sleep in Jesus"—an obvious reference to the resurrection. Paul is simply declaring that because God brought Jesus from the grave, we have a guarantee that He *will bring* sleeping saints forth in the same way at the time of His coming.

2 Thessalonians 2:6

"And now ye know what withholdeth that he might be revealed in his time."

From previous verses we learn that Paul is talking about the Antichrist being revealed. Apparently he had talked to the church earlier about some power that was preventing the full revelation of that man of sin. In verse 7 also, Paul refers to a certain entity who would cease withholding by being "taken out of the way."

Unfortunately, these meager clues do not identify the information that had been previously discussed with the Thessalonians. Paul's guarded language seems to indicate that it might be a politically explosive issue, and he avoided calling the restraining power by name.

Many believe that the epistle is referring to the authoritarian influence of the pagan Roman empire, which did indeed hinder the growth and development of the papal religious system. With its fall in A.D. 476, the way was cleared for a rapid world domination of the papal church, which continued until 1798.

2 Thessalonians 2:15

"Therefore, brethren, stand fast, and hold the traditions which ye have been taught, whether by word, or our epistle."

The Greek word translated "traditions" is "paradoseis," which literally means "things handed over" or "passed down." There were many traditions of men that were based upon error and false theories. These are heartily condemned in the Bible because they contradict or subvert the truth of God (Matthew 15:3).

But these traditions spoken of by Paul in 2 Thessalonians 2:15 were those things that had been handed over by Christ and that the apostles were now passing along to the world. Paul does not give a wholesale endorsement to tradition as such. He limits the traditions to which they should "hold fast" to those the church had received "by word or our epistle." This encompassed only the inspired teaching or writing of those who had received their message directly from Christ and were ministering to the churches at that time. Paul declared that if any person or angel should preach any other gospel than the one he had preached, "… let him be accursed" (Galatians 1:8).

1 Timothy 2:11-15

"Let the woman learn in silence with all subjection. But I suffer not a woman to teach, nor to usurp authority over the man, but to be in silence. For Adam was first formed, then Eve. And Adam was not deceived, but the woman being deceived was in the transgression. Notwithstanding she shall be saved in childbearing, if they continue in faith and charity and holiness with sobriety."

First it is good to understand that the word for silence in the original Greek does not signify total silence but rather "quietness" and "peacefulness." It is quite clear from Paul's statement in 1 Corinthians 11:5 that women were encouraged to pray and prophesy along with others in the congregation.

In his epistle to Timothy, Paul is addressing the reason for women to exercise only a supportive role in the church as far as speaking was concerned. Paul cites the creational model of Adam's primacy in the home and church. Because of being first in the order of God's creation, only the man was to be the authoritarian spokesman to the church.

Some have assumed that this counsel was based only on local cultural practices, but the text establishes God's own order at the time of Creation, before the resulting "curses" were pronounced on Adam and Eve. It is also important to notice that this epistle is specifically written to explain how things should be done in the church. Paul wrote, "These things write I unto thee … that thou mayest know how thou oughtest to behave thyself in the house of God, which is the church of the living God, …" (1 Timothy 3:14, 15).

The words of 1 Timothy 2:12 indicate that no teaching or speaking of women in church should "usurp authority over the man." Verse 11 says that they should be in "subjection." Again, this order of authority is not rooted in culture or natural abilities or inferiority but rather upon God's own order of creation. In verses 11 and 12 we have an inverted parallelism. What is stated positively in verse 11 is restated and amplified negatively in verse 12.

In summary, these verses teach that God established an order of authority for the church, where the man was to be spiritual director and teacher. Women would have important roles involving prayer, prophesying, and worship but were not permitted to exercise spiritual authority, which had been specifically assigned to the man.

1 Timothy 4:1-4

"Now the Spirit speaketh expressly, that in the latter times some shall depart from the faith, giving heed to seducing spirits, and doctrines of devils; Speaking lies in hypocrisy, having their conscience seared with a hot iron; Forbidding to marry, and commanding to abstain from meats, which God hath created to be received with thanksgiving of them which believe and know the truth. For every creature of God is good, and nothing to be refused, if it be received with thanksgiving."

The warning against a latter-day apostasy in these texts involves a number of heresies—following devils, forbidding to marry, and commanding to abstain from certain foods.

Perhaps the greatest misunderstanding has arisen over verse 4, where it is stated that "every creature of God is good." This means that every created thing has been made for a need and a purpose. But some suppose that every animal is therefore good to be eaten if it is properly prayed over and blessed by the prayer of thanksgiving. Not so! Praying over a buzzard or mole or bat will not make it fit for food. Then, in case anyone should come to wrong conclusions from verse 4, Paul hastens to add: "For it is sanctified by the word of God and prayer" (verse 5). Ah, now we know what sanctifies it as proper for the diet. The Word of God must approve it, and then the prayer of thanksgiving will sanctify it to be eaten.

It is helpful to note that the word "meats" in the original language is not limited to flesh foods. The Greek word "broma" simply means "food." Notice also that this discussion does not involve biblically unclean animals. Those meats which some had forbidden were meats "which God hath created to be received with thanksgiving of them which believe and know the truth" (verse 3). Now it is easy to find in the Bible God's description of the meats which He created to be received with thanksgiving (Leviticus 11:2-20). Those who "believe and know the truth" will receive those foods with thanksgiving because they are "sanctified by the word of God and prayer." God's Word is the truth. Only those who "believe and know" that Word will be led to those things that are "sanctified" and created to "be received with thanksgiving." Those who "sanctify themselves" while eating unclean meats will be destroyed at Christ's second coming (see Isaiah 66:15-17).

1 Timothy 5:23

"Drink no longer water, but use a little wine for thy stomach's sake and thine often infirmities."

The Greek word "oinos," which is translated "wine," may be either fermented or unfermented, depending on the context. But since alcoholic drink is categorically condemned in Proverbs 20:1 and 23:29-32, it is inconceivable that the New Testament church leaders would condone it.

There is nothing in Paul's counsel to Timothy to indicate that this "little wine" was fermented. Since Timothy had an apparent problem of digestion and also other infirmities, the recommended use of grape juice might well have been an effective dietary supplement.

The Bible writers also recommend the unfermented grape juice as a blessing to the body. "Thus saith the LORD, As the new wine is found in the cluster, and one saith, Destroy it not; for a blessing is in it" (Isaiah 65:8). The kind of wine that is "in the cluster" is nonalcoholic. Some authorities today urge the drinking of grape juice based on its rapid therapeutic ingestion into the system.

Titus 1:15

"Unto the pure all things are pure: but unto them that are defiled and unbelieving is nothing pure; but even their mind and conscience is defiled."

Paul is making a generalization about the saints and sinners. The pure-minded Christian looks for and finds the good in everyone. This obviously does not mean that God's people will label adultery, sinful conduct, or impurity by the term "pure." On the contrary, the Word of God pronounces a curse on those who equivocate and vacillate on matters of right and wrong. "Woe unto them that call evil good, and good evil; ..." (Isaiah 5:20).

Paul portrays the defiled sinner as one with a darkened mind and conscience who makes something evil out of the pure and good. Such men lived in the days of Noah and of Paul, and they still are found in the earth. Says the Bible, "... every imagination of the thoughts of his heart was only evil continually" (Genesis 6:5).

Hebrews 8:7, 8

"For if that first covenant had been faultless, then should no place have been sought for the second. For finding fault with them, he saith, Behold, the days come, saith the Lord, when I will make a new covenant with the house of Israel and with the house of Judah."

The question of the covenants has been greatly distorted and misunderstood. Briefly let us notice what the old covenant was not. It was not the Ten Commandments. Why? Because they did not wax old and vanish away (verse 13). They did not have poor promises (verse 6) and they were not faulty (verse 7).

Then what was the old covenant, and how was it ratified? It was an agreement between God and Israel described in Exodus 19:5-8 whereby the people promised to keep the Ten Commandments. It was ratified by the sprinkled blood of an ox (Exodus 24:7, 8). The poor promises of the people failed because they tried to obey in human strength alone.

In comparison, the new covenant was instituted and ratified by the blood of Jesus at His death (Hebrews 12:24; 13:20; Matthew 26:28). It went into effect when He died. "For a testament (covenant) is of force after men are dead: otherwise it is of no strength at all while the testator liveth" (Hebrews 9:17).

Now get this point also about the new covenant: "… Though it be but a man's covenant, yet if it be confirmed, no man disannuleth, or addeth thereto" (Galatians 3:15). This means that after the death of Christ, nothing could be added to or taken away from the new covenant. This is why Jesus introduced the Lord's Supper on Thursday night before He died—so that it would come under the new covenant (Matthew 26:28).

But ponder this question, and don't miss the significance of it. When did Sunday-keeping begin? All will answer, "After the resurrection of Jesus." Then it could not be a part of the new covenant. Nothing could be added after the death of Jesus, the Testator.

Hebrews 10:8, 9

"Above when he said, Sacrifice and offering and burnt offerings and offering for sin thou wouldest not, neither hadst pleasure therein; which are offered by the law; Then said he, Lo, I come to do thy will, O God. He taketh away the first, that he may establish the second."

Dispensationalists believe that the Ten Commandment law was a part of the law of Moses, which disappeared with the old covenant. These verses are used to support that false premise. The "law" of verse 8 is undoubtedly associated with the "first" covenant, which is taken away in verse 9. But did that law include the Ten Commandments? Those same sacrifices and sin offerings are described in 2 Chronicles 8:12, 13: "Then Solomon offered burnt offerings unto the LORD ... even after a certain rate every day, offering according to the commandment of Moses ..."

This makes it very plain that the law concerning those burnt offerings—the one mentioned in Hebrews 10:8—was called the commandment or law of Moses. It was a part of the old-covenant system that was taken away by "the offering of the body of Jesus Christ" (verse 10). But please note this important fact: The Ten Commandment law was not a part of that which was done away. Christ is quoted in verse 9 as saying, "Lo, I come to do thy will, O God. He taketh away the first, that he may establish the second." But let's get the full text of what Christ said from Psalm 40:7, 8: "Lo I come ..., I delight to do thy will, O my God: yea, thy law is within my heart."

Don't miss this point: The law within the heart of Christ is tied to the second (or new) covenant that was to be established. This is why in verse 16 of Hebrews chapter 10, the new covenant is described in these words: "This is the covenant that I will make ..., I will put my laws into their hearts, and in their minds will I write them ..." The law that was in the heart of Jesus and which did not end with the old covenant is the Ten Commandment law. Magnified by Christ (Isaiah 42:21), it was transferred from the tables of stone to the fleshly tables of the heart.

Hebrews 12:22-24

"But ye are come unto mount Zion, and unto the city of the living God, the heavenly Jerusalem, and to an innumerable company of angels, To the general assembly and church of the first-born, which are written in heaven, and to God the Judge of all, and to the spirits of just men made perfect, And to Jesus the mediator of the new covenant, and to the blood of sprinkling, that speaketh better things than that of Abel."

According to verse 24, Paul is here talking about the glories of the new covenant relationship as compared to the old covenant idea of human effort alone. Sinai is used to represent the old covenant (verses 18-21), and Jerusalem is used to represent the new. In Galatians 4:24-26, the very same parallel is made symbolizing the two covenants by Sinai and Jerusalem.

Some have interpreted these verses to mean that souls go immediately into the heavens at death to appear at the judgment bar. But please notice that these people come "to Jesus the mediator of the new covenant." Those who are saved in heaven will no longer need a mediator such as is described here. Sin will have ceased for them.

Paul is actually describing the life of a Christian here in this world as he begins to experience the joys of the new covenant relationship. Such a Christian comes to:

1. "Mount Zion ... the city of the living God." Peter speaks of the church in similar language: "lively stones, ... a spiritual house" (1 Peter 2:4-6).

2. "An innumerable company of angels"—descriptive of the angel ministry for the saints mentioned in Hebrews 1:7.

3. "The general assembly and church of the firstborn, which are written in heaven"—another description of the body of Christ on this earth. Paul spoke of his fellow laborers as those "whose names are in the book of life" (Philippians 4:3).

4. "God the Judge of all." This is parallel language to Hebrews 4:16, which says, "... come boldly unto the throne of grace, ..." and to Hebrews 7:25, which says, "... he is able also to save them ... that come unto God by him."

5. "The spirits of just men made perfect"—not disembodied spirits as some imagine, but the kindred spirit of Christian with Christian. Paul contrasts those who walk "after the flesh" and those who walk "after the spirit." But these are real people who have spiritual natures that are sanctified through the blood of the new covenant. Compare Hebrews 10:14: "For by one offering he hath perfected for ever them that are sanctified."

1 Peter 3:18-20

"For Christ also hath once suffered for sins, the just for the unjust, that he might bring us to God, being put to death in the flesh, but quickened by the Spirit: By which also he went and preached unto the spirits in prison; Which sometime were disobedient, when once the longsuffering of God waited in the days of Noah, while the ark was a preparing, wherein few, that is, eight souls were saved by water."

There has been considerable misunderstanding of these verses of Scripture. It has been preached that Christ actually descended into the lower regions of the earth and preached to lost souls who were in prison in some type of purgatory or limbo. This is very far from what the text actually says. Let's look at it closely now and get the real message of these verses. It says, "Christ also hath once suffered for sins … that he might bring us to God, being put to death in the flesh, but quickened by the Spirit: By which also he went and preached …"

First of all, notice *how* Christ preached to those spirits in prison. He did it by the Spirit, and that word is capitalized in your Bible. It actually refers to the Holy Spirit. So whatsoever Christ did in preaching during this period of time, He did it through or by the Holy Spirit.

With that in view, let's ask this: "*When* was the preaching done?" The answer is plainly given in verse 20: "when once the longsuffering of God waited in the days of Noah, while the ark was a preparing." So the preaching was actually done while the ark was being built—during the preaching of Noah to that antediluvian world. Now, one more question: "*To whom* was the preaching done?" The text says here "unto the spirits in prison." Throughout the Bible we find this terminology used in describing those who are bound in the prison house of sin. David prayed, "Bring my soul out of prison, …" (Psalm 142:7). Paul spoke of his experience in these words, "bringing me into captivity to the law of sin." What Peter is telling us here is simply that Christ, through the Holy Spirit, was present while Noah preached; Christ was there through the Holy Spirit to speak conviction to their hearts and appeal to them to come into the ark. There is absolutely nothing in this text to indicate that Jesus left His body during the time He was dead to go to any subterranean place to minister to wicked spirits. The three questions are clearly answered in the text itself: (1) that He preached by the Holy Spirit, (2) He did it while the ark was preparing, and (3) He did it to the spirits in prison, or to those individuals whose sinful lives were bound in the prison house of sin.

1 Peter 4:6

"For this cause was the gospel preached also to them that are dead, that they might be judged according to men in the flesh, but live according to God in the spirit."

Peter did not imply that the gospel was then being preached to the souls of the dead, as some teach. He said the gospel "was preached" to those who "are (now) dead." The preaching was done while they were still alive, and they will be judged on the basis of how they lived "according to men in the flesh," or while they were still alive.

Peter is undoubtedly talking about the Christian dead, because he refers to their living again "according to God (as God lives) in the spirit." In other words, they will receive immortality in the resurrection and will have a life that measures with the life of God.

2 Peter 2:4

"For if God spared not the angels that sinned, but cast them down to hell, and delivered them into chains of darkness, to be reserved unto judgment."

The word "hell" in this text is very unique because it is translated from a word that is used nowhere else in the Bible. The Greek word "Tartaroo" is certainly not the same as the "Gehenna" hell, which is referred to 12

times in the New Testament—always as a place of burning. There is no burning where the angels are confined,
because it is described as a place of "darkness."

In Jude verse 6 also, the fallen angels are said to be
"... reserved in everlasting chains under darkness unto
the judgment of the great day." Please notice that these
evil spirit beings are not now being punished, but are
kept in darkness, reserved until the day of judgment.
Both Peter and Jude speak of chains of darkness and
future judgment. Since evil angels are obviously still
functioning in deceiving people, we can only conclude
that these chains of darkness are the spiritual restraints
placed upon their activities until their final judgment
and punishment at the end of the world.

2 Peter 3:8

*"But, beloved, be not ignorant of this one thing,
that one day is with the Lord as a thousand
years, and a thousand years as one day."*

Please note that this verse does not say that one day
is a thousand years. It says that, with the Lord, one day
is as a thousand years and a thousand years as one day.
The Psalmist put it this way: "For a thousand years in
thy sight are but as yesterday when it is past, and as a
watch in the night" (Psalm 90:4).

It is important to observe that this statement is
made by Peter in relation to the promises of God. He
points out in verses 3 and 4 that some people scoff at
the promise of the Lord's coming. Then in verses 8 and
9 he emphasizes that even though a thousand years pass
by, the Lord doesn't forget what He promised. It is like
only a day to Him. In fact, in the next two verses Peter
affirms: "The Lord is not slack concerning his promise,
as some men count slackness ... But the day of the Lord
will come" (2 Peter 3:9,10).

1 John 3:9

*"Whosoever is born of God doth not commit sin;
for his seed remaineth in him: and he cannot sin,
because he is born of God."*

The key to understanding this text lies in the meaning of the word "seed." There is perfect assurance that the "seed" will provide total victory over sin. Who is this "seed" whose presence in the life can guarantee strength to obey? We find the answer in Revelation 12:17: "And the dragon was wroth with the woman, and went to make war with the remnant of her seed, which keep the commandments of God, and have the testimony of Jesus Christ."

The seed of the woman was the man child of verse 5 "… who was to rule all nations …" and "… was caught up unto God, and to his throne." Here it is firmly established that Christ is the seed. Further evidence is found in Galatians 3:16, where God said to Abraham, "And to thy seed, which is Christ."

Now we can grasp the beautiful truth in the Scripture before us. Those who are truly born of God do not willfully sin, because Christ is enthroned in their hearts. The only way they can choose to sin is by separating from Christ. In other words, the abiding presence of Christ and the willful commission of sin do not operate simultaneously in the same heart at the same time. Deliberate sin always separates us from Christ, and the Holy Spirit does not become a minister of sin. Contrariwise, those who are genuinely converted and have the indwelling of the Spirit will be able to overcome sin in all its forms and approaches.

This text does not mean that Christians are incapable of committing wrong acts (or else there would be no virtue in their being without sin); rather, their love for Christ constrains them from walking contrary to His will. The word "sin" here is in a Greek form that indicates a continuing process. In other words, even if they stumble into a sin, they will not continue such a course; but rather, will repent sincerely, repudiating any willful violation of God's revealed will.

1 John 5:12
(*See my comments on John 5.24*)

1 John 5:16

"If any man see his brother sin a sin which is not unto death, he shall ask, and he shall give him life for them that sin not unto death. There is a sin unto death: I do not say that he shall pray for it."

It is very important to understand the context of this verse. In the two preceding verses, John has talked about the assurance that believers' prayers will be heard and answered. Then in verse 16 he applies that promise to the specific case of prayer in another's behalf. In doing so, he discusses two classes of sin—one in which there is hope for the sinner, and another in which there is no hope.

In the first case, prayer could lead to the sinner's recovery and redemption, but the second situation held no guarantee that prayer would bring salvation. It seems quite apparent that the "sin unto death" is referring to the unpardonable sin. Those who are recognized as rejecters of the Spirit and are hardened by continual transgression would not be open to further conviction of their sin. In such a situation, the positive assurances of verses 14 and 15 could not be applied.

For all other cases, excepting the unpardonable sin, God will give life to the one who is being prayed for—contingent, of course, upon that person's repentance and acceptance of Christ.

Revelation 1:5

"And from Jesus Christ, who is the faithful witness, and the first begotten of the dead, and the prince of the kings of the earth. Unto him that loved us, and washed us from our sins in his own blood."

The expression "first begotten of the dead" has caused much perplexity. Obviously Jesus was not the first one to be resurrected. Besides Moses in the Old Testament, at least three individuals were raised from the dead by Jesus Himself.

There are two ways the word "first" may be understood. It can mean either first in point of time or first in preeminence. The President's wife is spoken of as the First Lady—not because she is the first lady who existed, but first in honor and pre-eminence.

Christ was "first begotten of the dead" because that resurrection took the pre-eminence over all other resurrections. In truth, all other resurrections had taken place or would take place by virtue of His triumph over the grave. His power to lay down His life and take it again (John 10:17) set Him apart from all others who had been resurrected. His was *first* in importance to such a degree that none other ever could have been raised without reference to His resurrection.

Revelation 3:14

"And unto the angel of the church of the Laodiceans write; These things saith the Amen, the faithful and true witness, the beginning of the creation of God."

The Greek word "arche," which is translated "beginning" in this verse, may have either an active or passive sense according to the context. The passive form would indicate that Jesus was the first created creature. But this is utterly contrary to scores of verses that portray Christ as eternal and coexistent with the Father (John 1:1-3; Hebrews 1:8; Colossians 2:9; John 10:30).

This means then that the word "arche" must be accepted in the active sense, which indicates that Christ was the one who initiated the work of Creation. In other words, Christ is the Beginner or Originator of Creation, and not Creation's first creature. He is the One who is acting, rather than being acted upon. Instead of being the One who was first created, He is the first One who created.

Revelation 6:9-11

"And when he had opened the fifth seal, I saw under the altar the souls of them that were slain for the word of God, and for the testimony which

they held: And they cried with a loud voice, saying, How long, O Lord, holy and true, dost thou not judge and avenge our blood on them that dwell on the earth? And white robes were given unto every one of them; and it was said unto them, that they should rest yet for a little season, until their fellow servants also and their brethren, that should be killed as they were, should be fulfilled."

Several facts appear from this symbolic account of the fifth seal:

1. These figurative souls of the martyrs are not pictured in heaven, but under the altar.
2. They show signs of being not merely unhappy, but tortured.
3. Quite contrary to Christ's instruction to pray for them which persecute you (Matthew 5:44), these saintly souls are represented as demanding vengeance on their persecutors.
4. This is an example of personification, when objects are assigned personal attributes. Such is the case of Abel's blood crying out from the ground (Genesis 4:9, 10). In this sense, the lives of the martyrs are portrayed as crying out for vengeance.
5. If this is not figurative language and if souls are disembodied, how do they wear robes? Obviously these verses are not related to any so-called "immortal souls" of the dead.

Revelation 14:10, 11

"The same shall drink of the wine of the wrath of God, which is poured out without mixture into the cup of his indignation; and he shall be tormented with fire and brimstone in the presence of the holy angels, and in the presence of the Lamb: And the smoke of their torment ascendeth up for ever and ever: and they have no rest day nor night, who worship the beast and his image, and whosoever receiveth the mark of his name."

The words "for ever" do not necessarily mean "without end." In fact, the Bible uses this term 56 times* in connection with things which have already ended. In Exodus 21:1-6, the Hebrew servant was to serve his master "for ever," but it was obviously only as long as he lived. Hannah took her son Samuel to God's house to abide "for ever" (1 Samuel 1:22), but she plainly limited that time to "as long as he liveth" (verse 28).

The term is clearly defined in Psalm 48:14: "For this God is our God for ever and ever: he will be our guide even unto death."

The desolation of Edom was to continue "for ever and ever" (Isaiah 34:10). Christ is called "a priest for ever" in Hebrews 5:6; yet after sin is blotted out, Christ's work as a priest will end.

According to these definitions of the term "for ever," the wicked will suffer as long as they continue to live in the fire. Then, as the Bible states, "The wicked … shall be destroyed for ever" (Psalm 92:7, See also Malachi 4:1-3.)

*If looking for these texts in a concordance, look under the word "ever."

Visit us online at
www.amazingfacts.org
and check out our online catalog filled
with other great books, videos, CDs, and more!

P.O. Box 1058
Roseville CA 95678
800-538-7275